LANDSCAPING *for* PRIVACY

LANDSCAPING *for* PRIVACY

*Innovative Ways to Turn Your Outdoor Space
into a Peaceful Retreat*

Marty Wingate

TIMBER PRESS
Portland / London

Published in 2011 by Timber Press, Inc.

The Haseltine Building
133 S.W. Second Avenue, Suite 450
Portland, Oregon 97204-3527
www.timberpress.com

2 The Quadrant
135 Salusbury Road
London NW6 6RJ
www.timberpress.co.uk

ISBN-13: 978-1-60469-123-8
Printed in China

Library of Congress Cataloging-in-Publication Data
Wingate, Marty.
  Landscaping for privacy : innovative ways to turn your
outdoor space into a peaceful retreat / Marty Wingate.
      p. cm.
  Includes bibliographical references and index.
  ISBN 978-1-60469-123-8
  1. Landscape gardening. 2. Gardens—Design. I. Title.
  SB473.W54 2012
  635.9—dc22   2011012384

A catalog record for this book is also available from the
British Library.

———————————————————————

FRONTISPIECE: Well-designed bamboo fences make attractive
barriers, and the material makes it easy for you to be creative
with the design.
PAGE 6: A fence can separate, but adding a buffer planting full
of flowers and textures creates a feeling of space without actually
taking up too much room.
PAGES 8 AND 9: A green roof provides not just more planting space
in a garden, but a way to help capture and filter stormwater before
it runs off into the municipal system.
PAGE 10: The large climbing rose 'William Baffin' softens the
landscape while creating a buffer between the garden and
roadway traffic.
PAGE 13: With good design elements and placement, a personal
garden space remains personal, even if it is on a mid-city rooftop.

For Leighton

CONTENTS

INTRODUCTION

Privacy is an overarching need in today's home garden, whether the garden is a small courtyard in a city condo complex, a shallow front yard along a row of houses, or a large space surrounded by a broad suburban lawn. Intrusions abound in modern life, and they assault all our senses. We long to create that one place where such disturbances are kept to a minimum. At home in our gardens, we want to feel protected from the untoward aspects of the modern world.

Living close together can result in community support and friendship, but noisy neighbors, annoying foot traffic cutting across your lawn, and marauding dogs (or children) can be too close for comfort and unwelcome in our personal space. These intrusions can take the form of environmental issues as well—consider a private seaside garden that evokes a romantic ambiance, until the destructive forces of wind and salt spray damage trees, shrubs, and flowers. Privacy and sanctuary can be difficult to achieve in urban and suburban communities: Whether a property is 5 acres or 3200 square feet, none of us wants to hear the neighbor's constantly barking dog or share a view of his (or our own) compost pile when we are trying to enjoy a cookout with friends.

Solutions to these and other problems are provided in this book. Here you will find ideas to soften, or buffer, the influence of poor conditions; to create barriers intrinsic to the garden; and to protect or hide a view by choosing the most appropriate screen. This book offers ideas for creating buffers for visual nuisances, noise, and environmental problems; barriers against wildlife and other trespassers, with information on fences, fence styles, and materials; and screens for hiding the everyday drab within the garden as well as the unwanted views outside the garden. In these

pages, you will also find information about hedges, hedge plants, and other materials and how to use them for problem areas in locations from large backyard gardens, to balconies and rooftops.

The design solutions in this book are not quick fixes, but practical, creative, sustainable ideas that will turn your landscape into an enjoyable extension of your home. These ideas for buffers, barriers, and screens are suitable both for city and suburban living. Thoughtful design makes these solutions an integral part of the garden that fits in seamlessly. Buffers that soften the impact of a nuisance can help build a landscape of increasing interest in form and texture. Barriers keep out unwanted views and noise, but they can also improve the visual appeal of a landscape, enhancing its vertical aspects. Screening hedges become more than shrubs planted in a line; they create a green, living wall, incorporating the design elements of sequence and repetition to pull together the landscape.

Out of sight, out of mind, we say; but our choices are broader than any easy way out. An evergreen hedge may provide an easy solution to screen off the view of your neighbor's hot tub, but it might not be the best idea for screening out traffic noise. Every spring, an army of arborvitae appears at garden centers everywhere. They provide a quick fix, but they are not necessarily the most appropriate answer to the question, "How can I make the ugly view go away?" Good design requires commitment. A tall, thin "wall" of hedge plants can disguise a chain-link fence, but if those plants grow 25 ft. tall and wide, you need to make the commitment to keep the hedge in check.

Some properties allow for sweeping solutions that use giant hedges and solid fences, but others within the close quarters of cities and suburbs have less private space with which to create extensive landscapes. Truth is, a long stretch of tall hedge or a big, blank fence does not suit most modern gardens. Neither is it appropriate for the size of most properties and the style of the home—be it Arts and Crafts or mid-century modern.

Hedges and humans share a long history, and the hedge in a large suburban or city property will continue to be an important element of the landscape, especially when it is used in a way that solves a difficult situation and adds to the artfulness of the garden. Hedges large and small, as well as fences and other design devices, can be used to enclose parts of the garden, to soften harsh effects, to provide privacy, and to disguise unwanted views without turning properties into little cells or eyesores.

This book offers information that can help you identify those aspects of the landscape that are not working for you. You will find creative, individualized solutions that fit your house, garden, and neighborhood style. In these pages, you will discover the best solutions to use as buffers, barriers, and screens for your property, landscape, and garden spaces to make them pleasant places to enjoy in solitude or to share with family and friends. Explore your options carefully, and you can improve your garden, home, and life.

BUFFERS

Softening the Impact of Nuisances

Like a pillow under your head, a secluded spot under a shaded canopy on a hot day, and the three place settings at the Thanksgiving table between you and your annoying cousin, buffers smooth the way, softening unpleasant conditions. Buffers in the landscape can ease or dull the offensive characteristics of nearby objects, traffic, circumstances, animals, or people in a variety of ways, absorbing the shock of life's more unpleasant realities.

A buffer does not remove the problem, but, like couching criticism in fluffy phrases, it makes the offense less annoying. Buffers also create the impression of distance: you may not add more actual space between you and the unpleasant situation, but it will seem farther away.

Buffers can be effective solutions in a variety of situations.

- The road traffic is too close—how do you escape?
- You need to put some distance between your property and the neighbor's yard, but you have little space to spare.
- The din of passing traffic detracts from the beauty of your garden and home.
- The noise from the barking dog next door, the kids at the playground on the corner, and the neighbor's loud music are driving you crazy.
- You have little or no garden space, but you need to plant something in a pot to provide a little privacy screen between your deck and a neighboring view.
- Your house is exposed to the hot sun in summer and could use some shelter during the winter.
- Your beachfront garden is getting burned by wind and salt.
- You need your own space, but so do the kids and the dog.

Nearby foot and car traffic might be too close to your front door, and noisy neighbors can be a source of constant irritation. As you seek relief from such nuisances in and around your own garden, patio, deck, or terrace, you may be tempted to plant a tall hedge or erect a solid fence to try to make the problem go away. But such overdramatic solutions will not suit every situation. A hedge may hide the unpleasantness, but it will not solve the problem. Those pesky irritations of city and suburban life will increase as people move closer and closer together in communities with condos, apartments, and houses on small lots.

You can use creative design ideas to buffer, or soften, the offensive elements that keep you from enjoying your home and garden. Using good design principles, you can create a buffer that reflects your personal style and contributes to the aesthetic of your property. You cannot create more space between you and what bothers you, but you can create the illusion of separation, which can work just as well.

In addition to manmade intrusions such as loud traffic or noisy playgrounds, natural intrusive elements can be softened by thoughtful selection and placement of buffers created with plants and structures. Whether the problem is the wind that whistles down the street and swirls around your small patio garden, the sunlight that heats up your dining room in summer, or the salt spray that blows up onto your property, you can choose design elements and plants that help alleviate the problems instead of merely hiding them. You cannot stop the wind, the sun will continue to shine, and children will continue to visit and play at the playground, but you can still keep your home and garden beautiful and comfortable despite these conditions.

PAGES 16 AND 17: Instead of a barricade that keeps the world at arm's length, consider planting an ornamental garden buffer between your home and sidewalk and street traffic.
PAGE 18: An island bed fills the empty space between the front yard and the road. The bubbling, mosaic fountain plays several roles, including masking street noises and attracting birds.
OPPOSITE: This *Clematis montana* does not block the view into or out of the home, but it forms a successful buffer between the house and the street and creates the illusion of separation.

VISUAL NUISANCES
Creating Buffers for Privacy and Sanctuary

One solution to the problem of visual nuisances is to cushion the effect so that the problem recedes into the background. A front porch too close to a busy street might not be the quietest place to sit, but sometimes it is all you have. You can lessen the irritation of traffic sights and sounds by creating a buffer: Plant a soft, billowing strip of low shrubs intermingled with perennials and bulbs between your porch and the sidewalk or roadway. Add a mixture of evergreen and deciduous shrubs to provide a year-round green strip and to let in some extra light during the winter months. Such a planting solves the problem and contributes to your landscape at the same time.

Using elevation to your advantage

If your house and garden sit atop a slope, you can easily create a buffer between your home and the jarring traffic on the street below. In fact, you can feel a bit of superiority as you look down on the city bus as it rumbles by: You feel above it all. On a slope, the effect of buffer plantings is intensified. Plant a mixed row of shrubs and perennials, or fill in the tops of retaining walls and rockeries with low, mounding evergreen plants such as rock roses (*Cistus* spp.), dwarf selections of Japanese holly (*Ilex crenata*), and evergreen blueberries (such as *Vaccinium* 'Sunshine Blue').

OPPOSITE, TOP: An elevated bed of terraced perennials and shrubs, instead of lawn alone, creates a sense of distance between the home and the street.
OPPOSITE, BOTTOM LEFT: A mixed planting strip, beautiful in all seasons, buffers the effects of passing street traffic without attempting to hide it. Even with no room for an effective sound buffer, the plantings help to alleviate the effects of noise.
OPPOSITE, BOTTOM RIGHT: A bus stop on the street just outside the front door calls for a buffer, not a barricade. This bountiful planting provides a buffer between home and sidewalk, and the plants enhance the home instead of hiding it behind a hedge.

Mounding shrubs for terraced slopes

Add a distance buffer by filling in terraced beds with a mix of evergreen mounding shrubs.

Chamaecyparis obtusa 'Nana', 'Nana Aurea', 'Nana Gracilis', hinoki cypress: Small mounding conifer with green ('Nana'), golden ('Nana Aurea'), and dark green 'Nana Gracilis') foliage. 3 × 3 ft. Full sun to part shade. Zones 4–8.

Cistus ×*hybridus* (syn. C. ×*corbariensis*), rock rose: Evergreen with dark gray-green foliage; pink buds to white flowers in late spring. 3 × 5 ft. Full sun. Needs sharp drainage. Zones 7–10.

Cistus ×*skanbergii*, dwarf pink rock rose: Dense evergreen with gray-green foliage; pink flowers in late spring. 3 × 5 ft. Full sun. Needs sharp drainage. Zones 7–10.

Ilex crenata 'Helleri', Japanese holly: Evergreen with small, dark green foliage. 4 × 5 ft. Full sun to part shade. Zones 6–9.

Ilex crenata 'Northern Beauty': Evergreen with small, glossy, dark green foliage. 4 × 4 ft. Full sun to part shade. Zones 6–9.

Pittosporum tenuifolium 'Golf Ball', golf ball kohuhu: Evergreen with dense green foliage and black stems. 3 × 3 ft. Full sun to part shade. Zones 8–11.

Vaccinium 'Sunshine Blue', dwarf blueberry: Semi-evergreen to deciduous with clusters of white flowers in spring, long summer season of fruit, and red and orange fall color. 4 × 4 ft. Full sun to part shade. Zones 5–10.

Vaccinium ovatum, evergreen huckleberry: Evergreen with dark green foliage and bronze new growth; clusters of white flowers in spring followed by fruit. 5 × 5 ft. Part shade to shade. Tolerates dry summer soil once established. Zones 7–9.

Using plants on a slope provides an inexpensive buffer against traffic, but you can go a step further by redesigning the slope. When steep slopes are terraced, the layers create additional space for more plants, and this seems to enlarge your property as well.

Landscape roses bloom for months on end beginning in late spring, and they last throughout the summer; they provide the perfect colorful buffer in a terraced planting. Look for selections such as the pale pink *Rosa* 'Radyod' (Blushing Knock Out); *R.* 'ChewMay-Time' (Oso Easy Paprika), with reddish-orange blooms and a bright yellow eye; and the pale yellow *R.* 'Radsun' (Carefree Sunshine). New and colorful hybrids are introduced by breeders every year.

Create your own elevation change in the form of a berm, an earthen mound planted with a variety of shrubs, perennials, and small trees, such as *Magnolia grandiflora* 'Little Gem' (to 20 ft.). Two to three feet of soil piled into a berm with a collection of plants serves as an effective buffer that provides just the cushion you need at the edge of your property, without taking up much space. Because a berm will be well-drained (as gravity pulls water through the soil mound), look for plants that, once established, thrive in dry soil. Consider planting French lavender (*Lavandula dentata*), English lavender (*L.* ×*intermedia*), bearberry (*Arctostaphylos uva-ursi*), shrubby cinquefoil (*Potentilla fruticosa*), and a low-growing selection of ninebark such as *Physocarpus opulifolius* 'Nanus', which make showy, long-lasting contributions.

ABOVE: A formal island bed floating in a sea of lawn creates a buffer between the front of the house—door and picture window—and the public right-of-way.

Many types of bulbs offer colorful options for planting strips.

Allium cristophii, **star of Persia:** Star-shaped, lavender flowers with 5 in. diameter heads. 20 in. Full sun. Zones 3–8.

Allium aflatunense 'Purple Sensation', **ornamental onion:** Red-purple flowers with 3 in. diameter clusters. 30 in. Full sun. Zones 3–8.

Allium 'Gladiator': Lilac-colored flowers with 5 in. diameter heads. 40 in. Full sun. Zones 3–8.

Allium 'Mars': Red-purple flowers with 5 in. diameter heads. 36 in. Full sun. Zones 3–8.

Chionodoxa forbesii 'Blue Giant', **glory of the snow**: Star-shaped blue flowers with white centers. 6–12 in. Full sun to part shade. Zones 3–8.

Chionodoxa luciliae: Blue, star-shaped flowers with light centers. 6–10 in. Full sun to part shade. Zones 3–8.

Crocus tommasinianus, C. chrysanthus, **early crocus, golden crocus:** Grassy foliage with small, cup-shaped flowers in white, lavender, and yellow shades in winter or early spring. 4–6 in. Full sun to part shade. Zones 3–8.

Narcissus 'Barrett Browning', **daffodil:** White petals with red-orange cup. 16 in. Full sun to part shade. Zones 4–8.

Narcissus 'Cheerfulness': White flowers with yellow flecks at center; fragrant. 16 in. Full sun to part shade. Zones 4–8.

Narcissus 'Geranium': White petals with salmon-colored cups; fragrant. 16 in. Full sun to part shade. Zones 4–8.

Narcissus 'Pipet', *N.* 'Tete-a-Tete': Bright yellow flowers; early bloomer. 6 in. Full sun to part shade. Zones 4–8.

Triteleia laxa 'Queen Fabiola' (syn. *T. laxa* 'Koningin Fabiola'), **triplet lily:** Purple-blue flowers in early summer. 24 in. Full sun. Zones 5–9.

Tulipa clusiana, **lady tulip:** Open yellow flowers with red backing. 10 in. Full sun. Zones 3–8.

Tulipa tarda, **late tulip:** Star-shaped white flowers with large yellow centers, early spring. 8 in. Full sun. Zones 3–8.

Buy and plant bulbs in the autumn. Plant them in clusters rather than in "shooting-gallery" rows. Let the foliage die back naturally before cutting it off.

Island beds and streetside plantings

As you stand at the curb, toes hanging over the edge, waiting for the "walk" light, and a delivery truck barrels by, you feel as though nothing lies between you and the noisy vehicle but air—and not much of that. But step back, stand behind a lushly planted garden or a row of shrubs, and you feel much less threatened by passing traffic.

A buffer planting within an island bed eases the tension between you and the street, whether you are standing in your front yard, sitting on the front porch with a cup of coffee, or looking out the picture window from your living room. An island bed creates an impression of distance without requiring a lot of room. Surrounded by lawn, an island bed floats in a sea of green grass. It can be any size you want, even using most of the space between the house and sidewalk or street if required.

An island bed on level ground provides much more of a buffer than lawn alone. Placed between your front porch and the street or sidewalk, a beautiful grouping of plants helps buffer annoying elements while affording you a pleasing view and preserving valuable sight lines—for example, you might want to keep an eye on the neighborhood or allow neighbors to keep an eye on your house when you are away. When the bed is placed closer to the sidewalk, the private area between the bed and the porch is larger. Plan the shape of your island bed to match your house and garden style: oval, round, or square for more formal settings, or kidney shaped or freeform for more casual landscapes.

In many neighborhoods the narrow strip of ground between the sidewalk and street is planted with grass, which can be difficult to maintain, because it is out of reach of the water hose and the ground is often hard and rocky. This area, called the parking strip, planting strip, parkway, or extension, is usually on city property, although the city relies on you for its upkeep. Take advantage of this extra space and fill it in with easy-care buffer plants to create a bit more distance between you and the street. Try planting low, mounding shrubs here, along with plants that thrive in dry soil.

Add spring and summer bulbs to the strip for seasonal interest—because spring bulbs usually go dormant in the summer, they will need no water. Many daffodils (*Narcissus* spp.) naturalize, returning each year for a new show. Bulbs require an application of an appropriate fertilizer when green growth appears and require little maintenance after flowering until the foliage dies back. Ornamental onions (*Allium* spp.) provide eye-catching early summer flowers that resemble floating orbs. Tuck in clusters of small bulbs, such as glory of the snow (*Chionodoxa* spp.), to add color low to the ground. Avoid planting hybrid tulips, such as the Darwin hybrids and parrot tulips, because their flowering show diminishes after the first year; save those for pots that can be changed out. Instead, choose tulips that are described as naturalizers, such as *Tulipa clusiana* 'Cynthia'.

Street trees

Street trees can be used as buffers to diminish the annoyance from traffic on the street, without blocking access or views. Choose trees that allow sufficient open space below the canopy, as most cities have regulations about this space to ensure that pedestrians can walk by without encountering low-hanging branches.

Trees with low branches, such as the flowering dogwood (*Cornus florida*), make elegant statements in the landscape with their multiple-trunked forms, but this charming characteristic makes them a poor choice as a street tree. Most cities have restrictions regarding street trees, such as requiring clearance of overhanging branches of 8 ft. from the sidewalk and 14 to 16 ft. from the street, for safety reasons.

City forestry or transportation departments can often provide a list of recommended street trees, or you can use a list offered by a nearby city. The list will include trees suited not only to your region, but those suited to the available space. If utility wires loom overhead, choose a short, round tree, such as the trident maple (*Acer buergerianum*) or hedge maple (*A. campestre*). For narrow roadways with no overhead considerations, choose a pyramidal- or conical-shaped tree, such as *Ginkgo biloba* 'Princeton Sentry', which grows 40 ft. tall and 15 ft. wide, and the European beech selection *Fagus sylvatica* 'Dawyck Purple', which reaches 70 ft. tall and 15 ft. wide.

Two-for-one buffer

Street trees planted between your property and the road cushion the effects of passing traffic, and they also act as a pollution buffer. Plants do a great job of capturing dust and airborne particulates from engine exhaust and manufacturing. In fact, studies show that streetside trees can reduce street-level particulates by up to 60 percent. The particulates settle onto the plants' foliage, and then, during the next rainfall, they are washed away.

Street trees also make use of the excess amounts of carbon dioxide produced by vehicles. Trees use carbon dioxide in the process of photosynthesis, absorbing it through stomata, the microscopic holes on the undersides of leaves through which plants "breathe." Trees then release oxygen as a byproduct of the photosynthetic process. In fact, a single mature tree can absorb up to 48 lbs. of carbon dioxide per year and release enough oxygen back into the atmosphere to support two human beings. Evergreen trees absorb more pollution than deciduous trees, probably because the dense foliage stays on the tree year-round, but any tree helps.

Remember that young trees of any species and cultivar should have some lower branches, which help increase the tree's caliper (trunk diameter). Remove these lowest branches as the tree grows; eventually, the tree will be tall enough for its branches to grow over the street and sidewalk without being in the way.

The size and shape of the tree that is best to plant depends on local conditions and city ordinances, but any street tree will buffer the effects of traffic—both vehicles and pedestrians. Old neighborhoods may luxuriate in huge shade trees planted decades in the past; these canopies overlap to cover the street, creating a ceiling of branches and leaves. Those same trees might not be recommended or approved by the city today, however, because they grow too big for the available space. The roots of trees too large for a space, for example, can grow so large that they break through or crack sidewalks and roadways, creating pedestrian and traffic hazards and an expensive problem to fix.

Informal hedges

Just as the billowing canopy of two or three trees between your house and the street can alleviate the irritation of the number 3 bus roaring by, an informal hedge on your property provides another solution to too much in-your-face reality. Informal hedges provide a cushion along your property line, without screening out a wanted view. You can plant shrubs in small groups or in rows using one kind of plant or a miscellany of evergreen and deciduous shrubs; the latter is often called a hedgerow. With little or no pruning, informal hedge plants grow into natural and lovely forms.

Some plants are not suited to formal shearing. When the natural form of a plant is intrinsic to its beauty in the landscape, it would be a shame to shear it into

ABOVE: A row of narrow hornbeams (*Carpinus betulus* 'Columnaris') is successfully used as a buffer in the strip between the sidewalk and street.

a narrow, upright, boxy, or round shape. For example, the spreading branches of the doublefile viburnum (*Viburnum plicatum f. tomentosum*) bloom with white spring flowers that march down the horizontal branches like epaulets; the plant would lose its magic, and the flowers may not appear, if it were sheared or pruned into a box or gumdrop shape. Because this viburnum can reach 6 ft. tall and 12 ft. wide, it's probably not a good choice for planting in a parking strip, but it could be used as a successful buffer between your home and the bus stop out front. These unsheared plants are best used in an informal setting.

Soft, mounding shrubs such as rock rose (*Cistus* spp.) and shrubs with arching stems and flowers, including species of *Forsythia* and *Weigela*, also suffer visually when pruned into boxy shapes. Leave the pleasing mounds alone, and remove only whole stems—as close to the ground as you can get—of arched growers.

Other shrubs and trees with horizontal branches range from the giant variegated dogwood, *Cornus controversa* 'Variegata', which reaches 25 ft. tall and wide, to the low-growing privet honeysuckle (*Lonicera pileata*), 2 ft. tall and 5 ft. wide. The small devil's walking stick tree, *Aralia spinosa*, with its huge compound leaves, tends to have a horizontal growth habit, as do shrubby Asian mahonias, such as *Mahonia* ×*media* 'Charity' and 'Winter Sun'.

Unpruned hedges of a single species are not quite formal or informal. The sameness adds a touch of formality, which is contrasted by the graceful arching or ascending stems in their natural form. Mixed hedges or hedgerows offer even more when used as a buffer planting.

OPPOSITE, TOP: A front porch and garden are well-protected by a hedgerow at the top of the slope, and street trees provide another layer between the house and the street.
OPPOSITE, BOTTOM: Mixed shrub plantings between the house and street, such as this planting of dwarf willow and bluebeard (*Caryopteris*), also provide habitat for birds and insects.
ABOVE, RIGHT: City and suburban bird life, such as chickadees, benefits from mixed hedge plantings that provide shelter, food, and a place to perch.

Hedgerows of mixed plantings

An ever-changing show of flowers, fruit, and foliage; birds darting in and out, with fledglings precariously alighting on branches; the full panoply of the seasons unfolding before you—all this, an entire garden, can be found within a hedgerow. Hedges screen out sights and help enhance privacy within. A hedgerow creates an exceptional buffer that softens the impact between properties or along a property line. Hedgerows are a mix of shrubs—some evergreen, some deciduous—that can be maintained in a more casual form than sheared hedges. For year-round interest, consider a hedgerow comprising two evergreens to every deciduous shrub.

Hedgerows often include plants native to your area. In the United States, consider including the California wax myrtle (*Morella californica*), native to temperate regions of the American West Coast, or sweet bay magnolia (*Magnolia virginiana*), native to areas of the East Coast. Or use "near-natives," such as Foster's holly (*Ilex* ×*attenuata* 'Fosteri', a hybrid of two North

American hollies, *I. opaca* × *I. cassine*), or non-native species suited to the site. The hedgerow's loose, natural form and varied species offers visual appeal throughout the year.

Designing a hedgerow for your garden is a personal decision with a variety of considerations. The evergreen strawberry tree (*Arbutus unedo*) offers winter flowers and fruit; plant it next to a showy ninebark, such as *Physocarpus opulifolius* 'Mindia' (Coppertina), with summer flowers and colorful foliage from the spring to the fall. Or, for a broader assortment of interest, intersperse these selections with tall Oregon grape (*Mahonia aquifolium*), which blooms in early spring.

Hedgerows offer seasonal delights: flowers turn into fruit with crab apples, mahonias, serviceberries, and snowberries; fall colors emerge from smoke bushes, which also offer colorful spring and summer foliage, such as yellow in *Cotinus* 'Golden Spirit' and purple-red in *C.* 'Grace'; and winter bare stems mix with evergreen branches. Planting a mixed, informal hedge avoids one of the biggest problems with hedges: empty spaces. When one plant dies, you can plant another without worrying about whether it will match the existing hedge perfectly.

As you choose hedge plants that provide interesting textures and colorful flowers and fruit, remember that the birds in your neighborhood will take advantage of the same plants. Hedgerows provide cover and food—from the nectar of plum flowers, fruit from chokecherry (*Aronia* spp.), and dried seed heads of ninebark. Birds also eat insects that hide under leaves and lay eggs in the plants; the larvae feed on the plants and birds feed on the larvae. Hedgerows also provide nesting space for birds and other small animals. Birds

need shelter throughout the day; evergreens, including conifers such as shore pine (*Pinus contorta* var. *contorta*) and broadleaf plants such as Carolina laurel (*Prunus caroliniana*), offer birds a place to hide when predator hawks fly by. A variety of plant sizes creates perches of varying heights, and the variety in bark lets birds such as the brown creeper find food as it makes its trek up the trunk. The longer the hedgerow, the more benefits you provide for wildlife, but even short hedgerows offer habitat.

A hedgerow fits into a small garden, too. With careful planning, a corner area or length of any city property planted in a hedgerow offers the same benefits as a hedgerow planted on a large property. Small hedgerows are similar to "remnant hedgerows" in the countryside, where only sections of old hedgerows survive. Hedgerows make good buffers, so-so barriers (depending on the plants you choose), and good screens, as long you are not hoping to screen out your neighbor's second-story deck.

When you are planning and planting a hedgerow, consider the shrubs' cultural requirements as well as your own design ideas or requirements. Perhaps you need a corner hedgerow or a hedgerow along one side of your property, 10 ft. in either direction—not as a buffer, but as a way to delineate the property line and attract a bit of wildlife. The more limited the space, the more carefully you must choose the type and number of shrubs you plant, always keeping in mind that some pruning for size will probably be required.

Pruning a hedgerow does not mean hauling out the hedge trimmer; hedgerow plants look best with selective cuts that keep the plants more compact yet allow their natural shape to reign. Use selective cuts to remove entire branches; removing even one or two branches can significantly change the shape and size of a shrub. If your hedgerow shrubs need pruning and you do not get to it in late winter, wait until after wildlife nesting season to get the job done and avoid disturbing animal families.

OPPOSITE: Red-twig dogwood (*Cornus sanguinea* 'Midwinter Fire') and beautyberry (*Callicarpa bodinieri* var. *giraldii* 'Profusion') do double duty as both a buffer hedgerow between two houses and as ornamentals that put up with seasonally damp soil in the drainage channel installed in the narrow space.

NOISY NUISANCES
Creating Sound Buffers

Sound becomes noise when someone perceives the sound as a problem. Using plants alone will not always solve a noise problem, but sometimes, when the source is out of sight, the irritation at the noise lessens (out of sight, out of mind). A hedge offers a psychological barrier to the sound, lessening our perception of it—and perception is everything.

Actual decibel levels (the units for measuring sound) and perceived levels are two different things. If you dislike the noise or the source of the noise, you consider it a problem. If, however, you enjoy hearing the

music from a neighbor's stereo speakers or a ball game broadcast on his radio, you might wish he would turn up the volume so you could hear it better. Your next-door neighbor, however, might wonder why a game has to be broadcast throughout the neighborhood. Traffic on a busy street that reaches 70 decibels may seem much louder to you than your favorite music played at 70 decibels, because you want to hear the music but would rather not hear the traffic.

When you live on an average to small city or suburban lot, you cannot eliminate the sounds created by traffic or your neighbor kid's garage band by using plants alone. Studies have shown, however, that sound decibels can be lowered using a dense planting of evergreen trees—but "dense" here means a row of buffering plants at least 16 ft. deep. For many homeowners, such a hedge would take up most, if not all, of the garden space.

The design of a garden or space can also worsen noise problems. Sounds are magnified by hard sur-

BELOW: Rustling leaves from trees, shrubs, and perennials can create an effective sound buffer between the house and street.
OPPOSITE: A large water fountain with splashing water helps to buffer the noise of a nearby freeway.

faces, such as concrete or flagstone patios and walkways, seating near the house, solid fences, and bare walls. Sounds from the outside bounce off those surfaces and become more annoying. Sounds created within your property can add to the problem if you position noisy activities too close to surfaces that magnify the sounds. You can, for example, site a basketball court on the opposite side of the garage, where the garage wall will bounce the sound the opposite direction from your bedroom window. Wall surfaces planted with noise-buffering plants provide an attractive visual element as well.

Buffer solutions to noise problems work in ways that do not eliminate the problem—you cannot stop the school buses from rumbling down your street or the din from a nearby highway—but you can find solutions to help decrease the annoyance.

Distraction as a buffer

State and federal transportation departments build thick, concrete sound barrier walls along freeways to reduce the noise levels at nearby properties. These sound barriers are effective, but none of us wants to look at one in our back yard. Instead of using such a drastic solution, the next best thing might be to change your perception of the noise by creating a distraction. Often, when the cause of unwelcome noise is out of sight, your irritation with the noise lessens.

Distraction plays a big part in buffering noisy nuisances. Mask an unwanted sound with a more pleasant one to divert attention from the noise and focus it on the pleasant sounds. The intention is not to compete with the noise, but to mask it sufficiently so that the natural garden sounds are the first to reach your ear, ahead of the traffic sounds.

WATER FEATURES AS SOUND BUFFERS

Unless you build an enormous waterfall, the sounds created by a water feature will not totally mask all outside noises. But you can create a large, recirculating water feature that offers the drama and the sound of a waterfall without requiring an accompanying stream or pond.

Many landscape designers insist that every garden must include a water feature, which embodies the very nature of an aural mask—white noise—while offering benefits to people and wildlife. Water features reflect light, brightening the garden. A fountain provides a source of movement, even on still days. In summer, sprays of water cool warm the air, and even the sound of water is cooling. Birds and other creatures bathe and drink from the water basin.

A water feature should be located near the listeners to provide the most effective buffer; position the feature on the patio, next to steps leading to the front porch, or just outside your bedroom window—somewhere between you and the unwanted noise. You can create multiple water features, even in small gardens, or install a large fountain to be viewed and heard throughout the garden.

OPPOSITE, TOP LEFT: A backyard water feature makes an immediate impression on visitors to the garden, and the sound of falling water can reduce the impact of unpleasant sounds.
OPPOSITE, TOP RIGHT: Place a small water feature near the listener, such as on a front patio, near a door and window.
OPPOSITE, BOTTOM: A fountain that makes use of various materials can create several water sounds, and varying levels increase the layers of sound.

Water feature tips

Consider a few pointers as you shop for a water feature.

The more points of contact the water makes, the more sound it produces. Make the most of this with a feature in which water falls from several sources and onto several levels before reaching the pool; or choose a fountain that shoots up 3 ft. and then showers the basin below with droplets.

Water falling onto a metal surface makes more sound than water falling on wood, concrete, or ceramic surfaces.

Because of the echo effect, water falling into a deep basin or chamber that is only partially full makes more sound than water falling in sheets down the side of a container into rocks below.

A sheet of water pouring into a basin makes more sound than water falling into a single spot, and water that falls another level into more water creates even more sound.

Features with less masking ability can still create a soothing ambience. Trickling bamboo fountains create a steady pouring sound—a constant flow similar to the sound created by leaving a faucet running.

Bubble fountains, in which water bubbles up from the middle of a sculptural feature, create light, cascading sounds; more sound can be generated if the water then drips onto rocks. The higher the burble, the more sound the cascade makes.

Small, recirculating water features do not need to be plumbed, but you do need to make sure the reservoir levels do not get too low to avoid burning out the motor. The smaller the reservoir and the hotter and drier the weather, the quicker that will happen.

In climates where freezing winter temperatures are the norm, birdbaths and other small water features can be kept flowing in cold weather with a specially designed heater, but large fountains may need to be drained and the pump removed to keep them from incurring damage during months of low temperatures.

Although many types of water features require little in the way of installation—you set it up and plug it in—other features are built to suit your garden and its style, whether that be an above-ground, ornate display in the Tivoli style or a naturalistic, seeping pond filled with reeds and water lilies. Provide power temporarily using an outdoor extension cord—just until you decide to go the rest of the way and bury electric conduit (which should be buried 18 in. below grade). In a sunny garden, use a solar-powered fountain to avoid the power dilemma; this works best in regions where sunshine is the norm year-round.

Because water features offer a vast array of sounds—drips, gurgles, tinkles, and gushes—use your ears as you consider which fountain to purchase or create. Listen to a variety of fountains before choosing one. You want to enjoy the sound of the water, not wonder if someone left a faucet running. The sounds created by water dripping into a shallow pool differ from the sounds created by water pouring into a deep basin. A single-level fountain makes less sound than a triple-tiered fountain.

A fountain in an enclosed patio area will create more sound than a fountain located in the middle of an open lawn—use those hard surfaces to your advantage. In an enclosed patio, the water sounds bounce off nearby surfaces to conjure up the feeling of a grotto or a Spanish courtyard. Let the water drip or flow into a half-filled urn to add some depth to the mix. An urn's shape—wider in the middle and narrowing at the top—provides more space in which the water sound can echo. For even more sound, choose a fountain that provides multiple points of contact for the spilling water.

BELOW: The sound created by a small water feature with a single point of contact will be amplified by using the surrounding hardscape as an echo chamber.
OPPOSITE: Water dripping from many points in a trickling fountain in an enclosed courtyard compounds the effect.

Mosquitoes and water

The good news is that moving water discourages mosquitoes from laying eggs—the brisker the water movement, the less likely the mosquito will lay its eggs. But if you are concerned about mosquitoes, vigilance might be your best defense.

Mosquito eggs require 48 hours to hatch and pass through several stages before reading adulthood 7 to 14 days later. The life cycle is dependent on the temperature: in warmer weather the cycle requires fewer days, and in cooler weather, more days. In small and architectural water features (as opposed to naturalistic ponds), this gives you ample opportunity to keep tabs on the water quality and the critters swimming in it. Flush out small water features if you spot eggs (stuck together and floating; they look like little rafts) or larvae (called wigglers) wiggling up and down from the bottom of the pool to the surface.

Mosquito eggs and larvae are the favorite foods of some natural predators, and a pond may attract them: frogs, dragonflies, and birds can all do their part to control the insects. You can install your own control by adding mosquito fish (*Gambusia affinis*), available at pond stores, which eat the mosquito eggs and wrigglers. Goldfish will also eat mosquito larvae and can overwinter even under ice, but if you live in a cold climate, consider mosquito fish as you do your petunias—annuals to be replaced each year.

The biological control Bti (*Bacillus thuringiensis israelensis*) is a bacteria that disrupts mosquito larvae development. You can add Bti dunks (doughnuts) or granules to your water feature. Bti does not harm birds, pets, people, or most other insects.

Buffers in pots

If you do not have room for an in-ground buffer planting, you can decrease the effects of pedestrian traffic close to your condo patio or mask traffic noise that wafts up to your apartment balcony by planting buffers in pots or planters. Consider grouping plants in large pots, and place them where they provide the maximum benefit. Or add a soft shrub such as a billowing hydrangea to a large pot on a shady patio for summer and fall interest. Even if your home has no patio or balcony, you can create a garden in window boxes or in planters lining the stairway leading to your door.

All plants need water, and you must be particularly vigilant about keeping container-bound plants sufficiently hydrated. During long, dry summers or extended vacations, make sure that someone will be available to tend to the plants. Use an automatic watering system such as drip irrigation, set on an appropriate schedule, especially if you will be away. Container plants should not overwatered, and if you use trays under your pots to protect a patio, make sure they do not collect too much water; standing water surrounding a plant's roots can damage them.

In addition to providing pleasing sounds, water features draw birds and other creatures to your garden. Position the fountain where it can be seen from inside your home to enjoy the show of birds splashing in the water—far better entertainment than any television offering. Water in the garden may also attract dragonflies, which eat mosquito larvae.

OPPOSITE: A carefully arranged collection of pots and concrete planters form a buffer between a front door and the outside world.

Rustling leaves as sound buffers

Although dense plantings of trees and shrubs provide sound buffers, many gardeners do not have the space to devote to such large plantings. Make the most of a smaller green buffer by choosing plants whose leaves rustle pleasantly in the breeze.

Think of the soft rustle of bamboo in the wind, which quiets, calms, and relaxes the listener. Clumping bamboo will grow well in large pots for years, and it spreads slowly when planted in the ground, making it controllable. Clumping bamboo species such as *Fargesia murielae, F. nitida,* and *F. rufa,* are hardy to Zone 6; *Chusquea* species are hardy to Zone 8. Running bamboo, on the other hand, will indeed run. If you plant a row of running bamboo along a fence or surrounding a

BELOW: A well-placed deciduous tree, such as a Norway maple (*Acer platanoides* 'Crimson King'), helps to shade the house in summer and allows the winter sun to shine onto the home through its bare branches.

patio, you will need to install a barrier at planting time or be constantly on guard for spreading plant rhizomes, and you might regret your decision, because it tends to spread out of control. Although you can plant running bamboo in big pots, you need to watch for rhizomes that can slip through a drainage hole and spread to open ground. Running bamboo leaves may provide pleasant sounds to distract your ears from unwanted noise, but the plants may also drive you to distraction with their robust spreading ways.

You can also achieve a pleasant natural sound of rustling leaves in the garden by planting deciduous trees as a buffer; enjoy pleasant sounds in summer as well as winter from the dry rattle of brown leaves that cling to branches. Many species of hornbeam (*Carpinus*), oak (*Quercus*), and beech (*Fagus*) trees hold on to some or most of their leaves during the winter, and the rustle of the dried foliage not only masks other noises but evokes a pleasant wintry ambiance. As new foliage emerges in spring, the old leaves fall. Allow the leaves to decompose on site, adding organic matter to your soil in the most natural way. Or gather them to mix into your compost pile.

Deciduous trees for a tight space

Use the rustling effects of winter foliage from hornbeam, beech, and oak in a narrow garden area by selecting from several cultivars.

Carpinus betulus, hornbeam: Crisp, green foliage with yellow fall color. Full sun to part shade. Zones 4-8. 'Columnaris', 25 × 10 ft. 'Fastigiata', 40 × 30 ft. 'Frans Fontaine', 40 × 20 ft.

Fagus sylvatica 'Dawyck Purple', European beech: Red-purple foliage. 70 × 15 ft. Full sun to part shade. Zones 4-8.

Quercus robur 'Fastigiata' (Skyrocket), English oak: Deep green foliage with golden fall color; some brown leaves retained in winter. 45 × 15 ft. Zones 4-8.

ENVIRONMENTAL INTRUSIONS
Dealing with Pollution, Sun, Wind, and Salt

Threats to sanctuary and privacy are not always in the form of eyesores or noise—sometimes the environment itself intrudes in an unwelcoming way. Find solutions to such problems by looking for good designs that suit your environment, your garden, and your needs.

Fragrant plants as transitory buffers

The sense of smell is the most subjective of all our senses: one person's favorite perfume makes another person gag; the smell of cooked cabbage that evokes memories of grandma for one person drives another from the house. This intensely personal reaction is only one of the difficulties in trying to buffer unwanted neighborhood odors.

You might think that the smell from the neighbor's chicken coop or dog run can be masked by planting some fruity-smelling rose or by letting the honeysuckle loose on the fence. But even the most fragrant plants, including honeysuckle, mock orange (*Philadelphus*), or hardy ginger lilies (*Hedychium*), can help only so much. A study on rows of deciduous and evergreen hedges planted around the vents of poultry tunnels found that the amount of dust and feathers blown into neighboring properties could be reduced, but the plants had little effect on the odor.

In addition, blooming shrubs are transitory, which means that the flowers appear in only one or two seasons and the scent is often affected by daytime or nighttime temperatures. Even more important to "odor-eating" plants is the role of wind. If you are downwind from the source of the smell, plants will not likely be of much help. The prevailing breeze is key.

The shelter of trees

BUFFERING HEAT AND COLD

Rays of sunshine are especially welcome on chilly winter days, as they warm the garden and brighten our spirits. Winter sun shining on your house helps warm up the indoors, too, and can actually help reduce your home's heating costs. On the other hand, indoor temperatures increase during the summer as the hot sun beats down on your house, resulting in higher energy costs from heavy use of the air conditioner.

You and your home do not have to be at the mercy of the cold and heat: Let trees and shrubs come to your rescue. Careful siting of plants helps reduce your energy costs and makes your house, and garden, pleasant places to spend time, no matter what the weather is like. In fact, studies have shown that a homeowner who properly places trees in the landscape can realize savings of up to 25 percent in heating and cooling costs compared to those costs in an unprotected home. A single deciduous tree can perform double duty by letting in sunlight during the winter and shading the sun-facing sides of the home in summer.

For best results, plant a deciduous tree at least 10 ft. away from the side or sides of your home that receive the most sunlight; this will offer the greatest benefit while keeping most of the falling leaves out of your gutters. Choose a tree with a round shape and broad canopy rather than a conical or narrow tree to maximize coverage. Tree growth rate is usually measured by its size at 10 years and again its size at maturity. For example, a fast-growing pin oak (*Quercus palustris*) at 10 years might be 20 ft. tall, but it will reach 70 ft. at maturity. You might be tempted to spend lots of money purchasing and planting a large and mature tree, but young plants establish more quickly than large ones and grow quickly into healthy trees—in time, the smaller tree at planting time can grow to a healthier tree at maturity.

OPPOSITE: A well-placed tree offers the garden and home the benefits of shade in summer.

Shade trees for every size garden

Not everyone has room for an 80 ft. oak, but you can still reap the cooling and warming benefits of a deciduous tree by choosing one that fits into your garden in sizes from 25 to 40 ft.

Acer buergerianum, **trident maple**: Mature bark is mottled gray, brown, and orange. 25 × 25 ft. Full sun to part shade. Zones 6–9.

Acer ‘Warrenred’ (Pacific Sunset): Scarlet fall color. 30 × 25 ft. Full sun to part shade. Zones 5–9.

Carpinus japonica, **Japanese hornbeam**: Neatly pleated leaves and red leaf stems. 30 × 25 ft. Full sun to part shade. Zones 4–9.

Cercidiphyllum japonicum, **katsura tree**: Fall foliage smells like caramel. 40 × 30 ft. Full sun to part shade. Zones 4–8.

Koelreuteria paniculata, **goldenrain tree**: Midsummer yellow flowers yield pink seedpods. 30 × 30 ft. Full sun to part shade. Zones 6–9.

Nyssa sylvatica, **tupelo**: Red, orange, and yellow fall color. 40 × 20 ft. Full sun to part shade. Zones 4–8.

Zelkova serrata ‘Village Green’, **Japanese zelkova**: Begins vase-shaped and matures to a round crown. 40 × 40 ft. Full sun to part shade. Zones 5–9.

In addition to planting trees for shade, you can also plant shrubs for added insulation. A ring of shrubs planted within a few feet of the house creates air space that acts as an extra layer of insulation, keeping in the heat during the winter and providing cooling shade during the summer. Try evergreen shrubs such as rhododendrons, boxwood (*Buxus* spp.), English yew (*Taxus baccata* ‘Rwandans’), sweet box (*Sarcococca* spp.), Japanese holly (*Ilex crenata*), and inkberry (*I. glabra*).

Trees and lawns

Most lawn grasses thrive in full sun. Under the shade of a heavy tree canopy, lawns will not fare well. As the years pass, lack of sunlight will cause the grass to become patchy and thin. In areas of heavy shade, give up the lawn and plant a variety of ground covers, plants, and shrubs that will do well in those conditions.

You may be tempted to plant a green carpet of Japanese spurge (*Pachysandra terminalis*), but *Pachysandra* and other ground covers that grow best in constantly moist soil do not grow well in the root-filled, dry soil under trees. Plants that spread well in dry shade (a recommendation as well as a caution) include Labrador violet (*Viola labradorica*, Zones 3–8), evergreen bigroot (*Geranium macrorrhizum*, Zones 3–8), and bishop's hat (*Epimedium* spp., Zones 4–9).

NOAA and prevailing winds

To learn about the prevailing winds in your area of the United States, check the National Oceanic and Atmospheric Administration's National Climate Data Center website at http://www.ncdc.noaa.gov. Search for "Climatic Wind Data for the United States." For information on the prevailing winds in other parts of the world, go to http://www.wind-finder.com or use a Web search engine to find one of many other sources of information.

Windbreaks

Urban canyons created by tall office buildings and condominiums channel the wind, which grows fierce as it races through city streets. Heavy winds can also be problematic in suburban and rural areas, depending on the landscape and climate. The wind's desiccating effects distress people and plants alike. Wind whips moisture away from plant leaves just as it does our skin.

If you have enough space in your garden, plant a row of evergreens—broadleaf or conifer trees—and other plants to provide a windbreak. Even small versions of tall trees will yield a benefit: A dwarf incense cedar (*Calocedrus decurrens* 'Compacta'), for example, grows to about 5 ft. high and wide; a well-placed row backed by several taller Port Orford cedars (*Chamaecyparis lawsoniana* 'Silver Queen') can also do its part as a wind deflector. A thick cuticle covers the leaves of most evergreen plants, which not only helps them keep moisture in, but protects them from being ravaged by damaging winds. Flexible stems of other plants, such as California wax myrtle (*Morella californica*), will bend, not break, in the wind.

Plants make a better windbreak than a solid fence or wall, because the plants allow some of the flowing air to pass through. When wind encounters a wall, it will find a way to pass above or around the structure. The turbulence created by the wind as it passes over or around a solid barrier can be even more stressful than the wind itself. Because plants allow some wind to pass through, they do not cause turbulence and instead filter the wind and reduce its speed.

A windbreak diverts the wind from five to seven times the height of the plants—in other words, a row of evergreen trees 25 ft. high can divert wind up and over for a distance of 175 ft. Plant your windbreak perpendicular to the wind and on the windward side of your property, like an army waiting to meet an advancing foe.

Plant a windbreak of two or more rows of plants to increase its effectiveness. The longer the rows, the more benefits the windbreak provides, but even a short row of three to five plants will help on a small lot. A mix of broadleaf and coniferous plants will do the job of deflecting wind—lifting it up and over your property—as well as provide habitat for birds and other wildlife. Add

OPPOSITE, TOP: Planted within a few feet of the house, a hedge adds a bit of extra insulation.
OPPOSITE, BOTTOM: Planting layers of plants as a windbreak can help protect your garden and home from drying winds.

a row of conifers, such as shore pine (*Pinus contorta* var. *contorta*) in a coastal area or Serbian spruce (*Picea omorika*), and a row of broadleaf evergreen or deciduous shrubs such as *Abelia grandiflora* (Zones 6–9), *Weigela* spp. (Zones 5–9), and *Philadelphus* spp. (Zones 5–9), for the inside areas of the windbreak, where you can also mix in perennials to add color.

OPPOSITE: Seaside gardens must be able to withstand wind and salt spray. Look to hardy plants such as lavender and ornamental grasses to provide interest and salt and wind tolerance
ABOVE: A seaside buffer is provided by an outer row of shrubs with a mixed ornamental border on the inside.

Salt buffers

Seaside gardens must often endure salty spray year-round, especially when winds are a constant. In cold regions, gardens suffer from salt spray from another source: Salt spread on the roadway as a de-icing agent, mixed with melting snow, can be sprayed into your garden by passing cars.

Excess salts harm plants in several ways. Absorbed by roots and held within plant tissues, toxic concentrations of chloride ions interfere with normal plant processes by changing the water content of plant cells. If a high salt solution is present around a cell, the water in the cell moves out to equalize the salinity on both sides of the cell wall—this is called *osmosis*. The osmotic pressure causes cell desiccation and reduces the plant's ability to photosynthesize. In addition, high amounts of salt in soil changes the soil structure and upsets the balance of nutrients available to the plants.

If you live at the seaside or along roadways that are salted in winter, you can plant attractive buffers using plants that resist or tolerate the presence of salt that can damage other plants in your garden. Consider planting salt-tolerant trees, such as the gingko (*Ginkgo biloba*), Mediterranean olive (*Olea europaea*), and Japanese black pine (*Pinus thunbergii*). Salt-tolerant shrubs include *Escallonia* spp. and the sea buckthorn (*Hippophae rhamnoides*). Lavender (*Lavandula* spp.) and many ornamental grasses, such as zebra grass (*Miscanthus sinensis*), also withstand seaside conditions. These plants can tolerate salt on their leaves and (always within limits) around their root systems without the considerable damage this causes to other plants. Also look to see what your neighbors plant in their gardens, or learn about the native plants that grow along the coastline in your area.

You can also look for clues that a plant might be able to tolerate high concentrations of salt. Plants with thick bark, such as the craggy, fissured trunk of a pine, or a waxy cuticle, such as that which covers the leaves of the mock orange (*Pittosporum tobira*), might help a plant resist salt damage.

Lists of salt-tolerant plants vary with regard to how susceptible a plant may be to the damage caused by salts—one list will label a plant "tolerant" and another labels the same plant "sensitive." The health of your soil, the maturity of the plants, and the amount of salt present all influence how plants will fare.

Deciduous trees and shrubs have the edge when dealing with salts. Without foliage and with minimal physiological processes carried out in cold weather, these plants may not be affected by salt during the winter. In climates where road salts are regularly used or where sea salts spray into your garden, try tough plants such as chokeberry (*Aronia melanocarpa*), Siberian peashrub (*Caragana arborescens*), serviceberry (*Amelanchier laevis*), and hedge maple (*Acer campestre*).

Few evergreen plants tolerate both salt spray and salt in the soil. Hardy conifers include Black Hills spruce (*Picea glauca* 'Densata'), Austrian pine (*Pinus nigra*), and mugo pine (*P. mugo*).

KIDS AND DOGS
Keeping Play at Bay

Visual buffers can also be used within the garden to separate quiet areas from play areas. Children should be a part of the garden, where they can be in charge of planting their own flowers or vegetables or help with weeding. (A penny a weed may fall below standard pay these days, but you can work out a system.) Children also need an area for play, whether that be a single sand box or the ultimate model in swing sets.

Create play areas slightly apart from a patio or outdoor seating area, where you can entertain or sit quietly with a book while the kids feel free to have fun in their own space. Surround the play area with fluffy border plants—be careful not to include thorny plants such as firethorn (*Pyracantha*), poisonous plants such as yew (*Taxus*), or plants such as spurge (*Euphorbia*) with foliage or sap that causes rashes on contact or rue (*Ruta graveolens*), which causes skin irritation. Also bear in mind the potential danger from bees attracted to the flowers you plant; weigh that risk against the benefits of planting a buffer with flowering and fruiting shrubs. A handy snack of thornless blackberries or low-growing blueberries, such as *Vaccinium* 'Sunshine Blue' or *V*. 'Northsky,' can provide a healthy summer snack, but the flowers of those shrubs are visited by bees. For very young children, or if someone in the family is aller-

Salt types

The most common road salt used in the United States is sodium chloride, but calcium chloride and magnesium chloride are also used. All are corrosive and highly damaging to plants. A less destructive (for plants) but more expensive alternative, calcium magnesium acetate, may affect water quality. If you live in a region where de-icing agents are routinely used on the roads, you can find out more about the products by contacting your state and local highway departments.

gic to bee stings, eliminate the flowering plants or confine them to one corner planting of flowering shrubs—away from the slide landing spot.

Dogs also need a space to play. As you consider a location for the dog run, watch where your dog lingers on you property. Planning a dog-friendly garden depends on the dog and the owner. Some dogs know their minds—they know where they want to go and the way they want to get there. Others are easily encouraged or trained to go the way preferred by the owner. Garden (and dog) size makes a difference, too. Gardeners with large holdings may not mind letting the dog run free, but homeowners with small lots may need to en-

courage, train, control, and persuade their dog to stay away from more delicate areas. Choose a safe space in the garden for a dog run. You may need to shift a rock or plant here and there to accommodate the dog's space. After you locate the run, you will be satisfied, the dog will be happy, and your valuable plants will be out of the way.

BELOW: Separating the children's play area from adult space does not mean putting the kids entirely out of sight. All family members should feel comfortable to play in the garden.
FOLLOWING PAGE: A dog run alongside the main garden provides a great running space with easy access to the rest of the garden.

BARRIERS

Effective Designs that Deter Invasion

The world out there can be tough, and you need a little space to call your own—with no unwanted intrusions, such as wayward animals or passersby cutting across your property and through your garden. Adding a tall hedge or fence around the perimeter of your property would serve you well as a barrier to intrusion, but walling yourself in is not always the best way to keep the world out.

A barrier can, however, offer a solution to a plethora of problems.

- Trespassers cut across the corner of your property and trample your garden.
- At night, car lights shine into your living room window.
- You are concerned that alley foot and car traffic will invade your property.
- You need a perimeter barrier for your rooftop garden or high-rise balcony.
- The neighbor's junk—and the neighbors themselves—intrude on your space.
- Dead ends or sharp corners have you worried that vehicles may end up in your living room.
- You want to create garden boundaries without walls—but are plants enough to keep intruders out?
- Uninvited neighbors are making use of your hot tub or swimming pool.
- Even welcome visitors do not belong in every part of your garden; you need a solution to help them find their way.
- Deer, raccoons, and rabbits are creating havoc in your garden—you want a wildlife-friendly garden that does not let wildlife ruin your space.

An effective barrier creates a welcoming ambiance while guiding, directing, and instructing. A barrier helps discourage foot traffic that tracks, tramples, and treads across your lawn or through your planted beds. Barriers can be used to keep trespassers out, but they also can be used to deflect or redirect visitors within your property or garden.

Barriers can be implied, rather than obvious, such as a planted berm that redirects foot traffic around a particular area, or a low fence that keeps dogs and kids out of the vegetable patch. Use a barrier to encourage someone to take a certain path—to steer her around a shortcut through a bed of emerging daffodils or lettuce plants.

PREVENTING CORNER-CUTTING

If you live on a corner on level property, you know that people passing by often attempt to cut the corner across your lawn or garden to save a few steps. Before long, foot traffic can wear a path through the corner of your garden. When people traipse across your garden or lawn, even a small corner of it, it can seem like an invasion. You can discourage people from cutting that corner without installing a prickly hedge or a tall fence.

Berms as barriers

Properties that rise above the sidewalk level hold an advantage, because the retaining wall or rockery between the property and sidewalk creates an excellent barrier that discourages people from cutting through your property. But even if your lot is flat from sidewalk to front door, you can create elevation and provide a barrier by building a small rock garden or berm between your property and the sidewalk or street.

PAGE 52: A terraced slope leading to the front door uses a variety of barriers created with several materials, including boulders, trees and shrubs, and an attractively designed fence. The way is easily traversed, but the concept is clear.

OPPOSITE, TOP LEFT: A dense planting provides a screen and a barrier for pedestrians who might consider cutting the corner.

OPPOSITE, TOP RIGHT: A low rock wall, trellis, and plants form a barrier that matches the home's modern style and creates a colorful garden space

OPPOSITE, BOTTOM: A fence and pergola establish the property line, softened by a cluster of shrubs and small trees planted in front to discourage pedestrians from cutting the corner.

Although city ordinances may prohibit you from building a 5 ft. high berm or earthen wall close to the street at the edge of your property, you can probably build a berm high enough to create an efficient barrier. A berm is nothing more than a raised bed, usually freeform in shape, with sloping sides. When a berm is placed at a corner or along a property line, it discourages trespassing. When planted with trees, shrubs, grasses, and perennials, a berm becomes a screen as well as a barrier.

To prevent corner-cutters, build a berm about 2 ft. high that extends several feet along the sidewalk at the corner of your lot. The sidewalk will become a far more attractive path for pedestrians, and the berm will discourage or prevent them from taking a shortcut through your yard.

Add height to a corner berm by planting shrubs and small trees, such as a cultivar of flowering and fruiting serviceberry (*Amelanchier ×grandiflora* 'Princess Diana'), red-leaved smoke bush (*Cotinus* 'Grace'), or a selection of Japanese maple (such as *Acer palmatum* 'Shishigashira'). Accompany small trees with other plants to increase the barrier's effectiveness. Add mounding plants, including small conifers such as dwarf hiba cedar (*Thujopsis dolabrata* 'Nana') and dwarf western red cedar (*Thuja plicata* 'Whipcord'), and small, flowering shrubs such as *Spiraea japonica* 'Gold Mound'. Ornamental grasses contribute to the berm barrier, too—including evergreen varieties such as blue oat grass (*Helictotrichon sempervirens*) and herbaceous types such as variegated feather reed grass (*Calamagrostis acutiflora* 'Overdam').

ABOVE: A few fence panels and well-placed plants direct pedestrians around the corner, discouraging them from cutting across. This arrangement provides a barrier that is low enough not to block drivers' or pedestrians' views of other vehicles and pedestrians.

Plants and structures

A solid fence around your property says "Keep out," but a variety of plantings added strategically, either alone or surrounding a fence or similar structure, invites compliments from passersby on the color, texture, and year-round beauty, while deterring trespassing. A lasting arrangement of plants also serves to anchor the corner and visually establishes the property boundaries. Instead of a flat lawn that runs into a flat sidewalk into a flat street, a diversely planted corner offers a colorful point of interest.

For this corner show, the planting should be substantial, dense, and attractive throughout the year. Include small conifers such as *Chamaecyparis obtusa* 'Gracilis' or one of the many lovely hinoki cypress selections, surrounded by evergreen shrubs such as variegated boxwood (*Buxus sempervirens* 'Aureovariegata') and low-growing privet honeysuckle (*Lonicera pileata*), and finished with hardy geraniums and bulbs. In addition to adding plants, set a few fence panels at the corner and along each side as a more permanent barrier. Judiciously employed fence panels mixed with plants can provide a more pleasant aesthetic than a traditional fence.

Prebuilt fence panels purchased at a lumber or hardware store come in various lengths and heights; how many you use depends on how much space exists between sidewalk and house and how much space you want to devote to the corner barrier. If your house or condo is close to the sidewalk, two 6 ft. wide panels could dissuade trespassers, but depending on available space, you may be able to use three or more panels. Add a few low shrubs or tall grasses at either end to emphasize the barrier and to deemphasize the abrupt edges of the fence.

You can also install fence panels on your corner without including a panel in the middle, leaving an open area between panels for visual clearance or for more plants. Add a few low-mounding shrubs, a conical evergreen for that exclamation point, and a clump or two of bulbs. A well-designed middle planting will discourage corner-cutters, and the fence panels will discourage people from walking through your yard.

Building and maintaining a berm

Purchase a soil mix for the berm, such as a "3-way" or "5-way" mix, which comprises subsoils, sand, composted yard waste, sawdust, and manure. (Or, if you happen to be digging a large hole elsewhere in your garden, you can transfer soil to the berm.) Many soil product companies offer calculators on their websites to help you determine how much soil you will need for an area. Build the berm about twice as high as you want, because the soil will start out fluffy with lots of air pockets and will continue to settle for a season or two.

Firm the soil in place so that the plants' roots can get a good grip as they grow. Purchase or rent a lawn roller, a hollow drum that you fill with water, to compact the soil and save yourself a little time. Roll this over the top and down the sides of the berm to firm up the soil and eliminate large air pockets.

The berm will be well drained—perhaps too well drained. Gravity will pull the water through the soil, and that may cause it to dry quickly around the plants' roots zones. A targeted irrigation system, such as drip emitters, will deliver the water where it needs to go without wasting a drop. If an in-ground sprinkler system is installed in your front lawn, you might need to reconfigure the system, and you must move or remove any sprinkler heads that will be buried by the berm. To establish new berm plants and provide a short-term irrigation system, snake a soaker hose through the bed, where it will slowly ooze water into the soil.

Lattice fencing or other types of openwork fences make a lighter barrier that still does the job. Add plants on both sides of an openwork fence, and add a vine that winds in and out of the openings. As a finishing touch, install decorative finials or post caps on the fence posts.

LIVING FENCES

Living barriers may not be impenetrable, but they will discourage people and animals from trespassing. Carefully placed plantings keep trespassers out while adding more greenery inside the garden. A thickly set hedge acts as a deterrent, especially when the stems of the shrubs and trees mature to form a woven barricade. But a living fence is more than just another hedge.

Planted barriers can include a variety of trees and shrubs that grow into a permanent structures. Plant several trees or shrubs in a row to form a division between a patio and vegetable garden or as a railing along a walkway leading to the front door. Or espalier trees and shrubs to create living barriers.

Espalier barrier

Espaliered trees and shrubs are shaped into two-dimensional forms, usually with tiered horizontal branches, and a row of espaliered plants can provide as a living barrier. Many types of trees and shrubs can be espaliered, but fruit trees are common. Espaliered apples and pears can be used to create a living fence along a sidewalk—if you are willing to share the fruit.

Many nurseries sell young apple and pear trees that have been espaliered (and many grafted forms sport two or three varieties of fruit on one tree). If you want to do it yourself, look for plants that already have a two-dimensional structure, with branches that grow more or less horizontally in opposite directions. After you plant the trees, use a series of cables and a framework to support the branches. As the plants mature, the branches become strong enough to stand alone without support, and you can remove the framework.

Other types of shrubs to espaliered and use as a living fence include camellias (such as *Camellia sasanqua* and *C. japonica*), viburnums (*Viburnum* spp.), and thorny pyracantha (*Pyracantha* spp.) and quince (*Chaenomeles* spp.). Espaliered plants need regular pruning to retain their features. The best time to prune is often in late winter, with a trim just after flowering. *Camellia sasanqua*, a fall- and winter-flowering evergreen shrub, should be pruned only after flowering to maintain next year's flower buds.

Some vines can be trained along fences, but they require support and cannot stand alone. If you have visited a vineyard, you have seen grape vines trained along wires or fences; grape vines are often trained to grow onto a fence or an arbor in home gardens, too. The same is true for wisteria, the rambling and beautiful flowering vine; when trained along a fence, a wisteria will not only provide fragrant flowers, but its branches will provide a living barrier (and think about how much easier it will be to prune a head-high wisteria instead of one that grows over the roof).

BELOW: Cordon, candelabra, and fan shapes are only a few of the many ways to espalier a tree or shrub.
OPPOSITE, TOP: Apple and pear trees trained into espaliers serve as a barrier as the branches mature and intertwine.
OPPOSITE, BOTTOM: A thick planting of prickly pear cactus (*Opuntia* spp.) will deter trespassers, but be careful where you plant them.

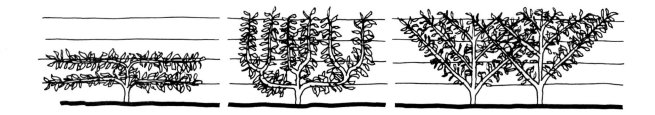

Thorny plant barriers

A CAUTIONARY TALE

Hedges of thorny or prickly plants can be used as efficient barriers—between the house and the alley, at the base of a window, or any place you worry about a trespasser gaining access. A thorny hedge will deter man and beast from entering your domain. But be careful where and how you plant a barrier hedge or even that single prickly plant. The thorns of plants such as pyracantha and quince will stick you and catch on your clothes as you prune and train the branches, and if they are grown too close to a walkway, innocent passersby can get injured as well.

Keeping trespassers out using spiny or prickly plants is one thing, but if you plant them too close to a place where you will need access, such as in front of a crawl space, a gas meter, or a water shut-off valve, you will resent those thorns, spines, or prickles that grab, stick, and scratch.

In dry, sunny regions such as the American Southwest, a collection of agaves, such as the *Agave parryi* (Zones 9–11), with its black-spine-tipped leaves, planted under a window would repel intruders on sight—or on first stab. Spiny thickets can also be formed using several dwarf barberries set close together; try the red-leaved selection *Berberis thunbergii* 'Crimson Pygmy' (Zones 4–9) or the coral-flowered *B. stenophylla* 'Corallina Compacta' (Zones 6–9). Note that barberries hide spines under their leaves; keep this in mind to avoid a painful surprise. Climbing thorny plants, such as climbing roses and Bougainvillea (Zones 9–11), can work their way up trees and trellises by hooking their downward-facing thorns onto the bark or wood. Trespassers will find it difficult to avoid their thorns.

When placing prickly plants, consider the size of the mature plants and the space available; these are the same considerations you would give when planting any hedge. You might enjoy the stained-glass look of the large red thorns on the winged rose (*Rosa sericea* subsp. *omeiensis* f. *pteracantha*, Zones 6–9), especially when they are lit from behind, but if its growth habit—8 ft. of stems that shoot up from the ground—is too much for outside your breakfast nook window, you will soon be cursing those thorns as you must continually prune the stems away. Always consider how tall and wide a plant will grow, and how much maintenance will be required to keep it a reasonable size, before you plant it.

Rooftop barriers

A rooftop garden gives you access to the natural world amid a sea of tall buildings, but if you get too close to the edge, although you may not actually be toppling over, it might feel that way. A rooftop barrier helps you feel safe on solid ground.

Both fencing and plants can be used to enclose a rooftop garden. A fence barrier alone would do the trick, but a rooftop is the perfect place for a garden; with free sunshine, rain, and space, adding living, breathing plants to the cityscape makes sense. Plant small trees in large planter boxes; arrange a climbing rose against the fence; or grow grapes and other vines that suit that full-sun exposure. A well-installed rooftop barrier will keep you safe, and the plants you add will increase the sense of safety, because you will not be able to see over the edge quite as easily.

PERMANENT FENCES

When you consider a property barrier, your first thoughts might be of a fence or wall—something tall and strong that promises to keep out all unwanted intruders and intrusions. Your next thoughts might be questions that come tumbling together: What kind of fence do I need? Do any restrictions prohibit me from building it? What materials should I use? Once you start looking at materials, your options might seem endless; you need not settle for less than the best for your garden.

Decorate your landscape with a fence that entertains as well as excludes. Look beyond the mundane: search books, comb through magazines, and wander the neighborhood until you see something you like. A suitable fence style may be available off the shelf, or you could modify a prebuilt fence to fit your own house and garden style. You can design and build the fence yourself or hire someone to build it for you. Your choice can complement the style of your house, or it could be quirky enough to stand apart and make a statement without looking out of place—an Asian style bamboo fence might not work outside a colorful Victorian painted lady, for example. To get an idea of how a fence design will look, place tracing paper over a photo of your house and draw a few fence designs on the paper.

A plain-Jane fence serves as an effective barrier, but it lacks visual interest. Enhance a plain fence to create more interest in your garden by adding ornaments, finials, or post caps, whether the style is formal or whimsical. Envision your fence from the inside and outside to imagine possibilities for enhancement.

With a typical solid wood fence, the cross pieces, or rails, that run from post to post and to which boards are attached, are located on one side of the fence, and the clear panels face the other side. That means either you or everyone else will be looking at the "back side" of the fence. If you want to avoid this situation, stagger boards on either side of the rails to show a finished face on the inside as well as the outside.

To add a little light to a plain fence, inset one or two panels of fencing into the garden by about 3 ft. or stagger the panels. The inset breaks up the visual line and offers another great place to add plants that provide a colorful skirt. Use the inset panels as backdrops

How high the fence?

Before you build a fence, check local restrictions. If you live within the city limits, fence-height restrictions are probably imposed, but even unincorporated areas might have restrictions. Height restrictions vary slightly from municipality to municipality, but most cities require that fences near roadways be no higher than 4 ft. with a setback of several feet between the street or alley and the start of the fence. The setback is measured from the property line located on the house side of the sidewalk; it does not start at the curb. Fences that run perpendicular to the street—such as between two properties—may need to stay at 3 or 4 ft. for some stated length, such as 15 ft., and then can be taller. Fences along the back of a property are usually restricted to 6 to 8 ft. in height.

Several other factors can affect how you build your fence.
- You may need to obtain a building permit to install a fence.
- When measuring the height of a fence on a berm, the berm is included in the height.
- Street corners have what is called a vision triangle; fences cannot usually be built to the corner but must be set back several feet.

for flowering shrubs with an upright form, such as redvein enkianthus (*Enkianthus campanulatus*); a round form, such as the bridal wreath spirea (*Spiraea prunifolia*); or a canelike grower, such as heavenly bamboo (*Nandina domestica* 'Monum' [Plum Passion]).

OPPOSITE, TOP: Municipal restrictions might limit the height of front fences to as little as 3 ft., but even a short fence can serve as a successful and attractive barrier.
OPPOSITE, BOTTOM: Although streetside fences must be kept low, taller fences are allowed in an alley to provide security as well as space for more plants.

Fence styles

Fencing options are abundant, and you can choose from a variety of materials and styles: split rail for a ranch house, pickets for Cape Cod, ornate balustrades for Palladian revival, or bamboo for Asian. Custom design a fence and have it built for you, or purchase ready-made solid or lattice-topped fence panels and dig your own post holes. The style and the materials you choose for a fence determine how secure and strong the barrier will be. A fence can be a lightweight barrier that lets people know where they should not walk, or it can be a barricade that ensures that nobody can trespass onto your property.

Barriers for pools and hot tubs

The "attractive nuisance doctrine" states that homeowners can be held legally responsible for injuries incurred on their property and must "exercise reasonable care" to keep children out of danger posed by the artificial conditions created on the property. The most obvious types of artificial conditions in the backyard landscape are swimming pools and hot tubs.

Keeping your hot tub and pool locked up can involve some serious thought—and cost. You can purchase locking covers for hot tubs, and automatic pool covers are also available, but their cost and maintenance may be more than you can handle. On the other hand, manually adding a childproof pool covering every time you are not outdoors to monitor its use is nearly impossible, because, after all, the covering is required for an entire season, not just for an hour or two.

Barriers—especially sturdy fences and dense hedges—exclude the unwanted visitor and can help keep neighborhood children safely outside the potentially dangerous area in your yard (and might help ease your mind). Childproofing your entire property is impossible, but providing reasonable barriers to features that can attract children makes sense from both legal and moral standpoints.

OPPOSITE, TOP: Black-eyed Susans (*Rudbeckia*) and sunflowers decorate both sides of an openwork fence; the fence serves a low barrier, and the flowers add color and soften the effect.
OPPOSITE, BOTTOM: The pattern of bamboo foliage is gracefully duplicated in a metal fence.
LEFT: Stone panels are set in a pattern to avoid the monotony of a typical fence using typical materials. Shrubs and vines (here, kiwi, *Actinidia kolomikta*) complement the design and contribute to the barrier.

When considering a fence, first determine its purpose. You probably do not need to build a fortress to keep out trespassers. Even an openwork fence serves as a barrier that discourages trespassing, while allowing you to wave at your neighbors or keep an eye out for suspicious activities. Openings in a fence allow light and air into your garden; plant vines that entwine in and out of spaces or shrubs that send out flowers to soften the look. If you need a more solid, impenetrable fence because of hazards or other issues (such as a swimming pool), consider creating a tall fence from metal, brick, or another sturdy material.

Properties at the end of a dead-end street or those that face a street corner suffer not from people trespassing, but from the continual, annoying flash of headlights from passing cars at night. A dense hedge or fence can help reduce the amount of light that shines into your home, but a solid fence or wall will actually deflect the light. Build a solid concrete or brick wall, and you also protect your home from a potential catastrophe should an out-of-control driver head your direction.

You should also consider slope when planning a fence project. A picket fence that runs along a hill, following the slope with each picket for a casual cottage look, looks sloppy. For a more modern, sophisticated take, build the fence so that each panel steps down the slope. This creates a clean, orderly look as each panel incorporates the important design element of repetition.

Fence materials

The materials used in a fence should complement the materials used in your house as well as your garden. A wealth of sustainable fence materials exist that will suit your home, style, and budget. You can choose fencing materials of natural wood, bamboo, bricks, or stone—all long-lasting materials manufactured from new or recycled materials. To choose wisely, ask yourself a few questions: Is the material from a renewable source? Will it end up in the landfill, or will it naturally biodegrade? Is the material manufactured locally? Is it long-lasting? Is it cost-effective? Does it require a great deal of maintenance?

Just say no to plastic and vinyl

Look to long-term goals of improving your property and contributing to the environment, rather than opting for a quick fix such as installing a plastic or vinyl fence. Plastic and vinyl fences look unnatural, because they are, and they can be difficult to fit into a natural landscape. Why surround a beautiful, living garden with unattractive plastic? The materials used to create these fences are nonrenewable and, when discarded, these panels will eventually end up in a landfill, where they will never degrade. In addition, the manufacturing of plastic and vinyl is a source of pollution and a drain on the ecosystem that uses precious resources.

WOOD FENCES

Wood fencing can be used with or without a finish such as a paint or stain. If you choose to paint or stain the fence, choose nontoxic brands that will not leach toxic materials into the soil. Some states, such as California, actually prohibit you from using toxic exterior stains because they leach poisons into the soil and water systems.

Many types of wood are available for fencing, but the most sustainable choice is to use lumber from trees that grow in your region and that are harvested in a way that does not endanger the species or its habitat. The native species might be redwood in California, Eastern red cedar or black locust in the Midwest and eastern parts of the United States, or Western juniper and Western red cedar in the U.S. Northwest.

OPPOSITE, TOP: As the elevation changes, so does the height of the fence, but in this case, it does so in stages, panel by panel, maintaining a clean line and appearance.
OPPOSITE, BOTTOM LEFT: On a sloping property, you can step down the fence in sections. Plant low-maintenance grasses, perennials, and shrubs to soften the look.
OPPOSITE, BOTTOM RIGHT: Cottage gardens of mixed flowers call for a picket fence.

Some tropical woods are sustainably grown as a crop and used to make durable, and often beautiful, fencing. Ipé (also called ironwood), for example, is grown and harvested in Brazil and Central America. Although it is labeled as "sustainable" wood, the fossil fuels required to ship the lumber to your locality might make you pause to reconsider that label. Native and tropical woods can be certified as sustainable in several different ways. The Forest Stewardship Counsel (www.fscus.org), a group that helps coordinate international forest standards, allows companies that meet its requirements to include its label on their wood products. The Rainforest Alliance (www.rainforest-alliance.org) offers its SmartWood designation in the same way.

If you want to use truly sustainable and local lumber, build your fence from reclaimed lumber milled from trees removed during development. Many companies are turning trees that would have been trashed into furniture and garden products. As an alternative, check online sources to look for used fencing. Now that is true sustainability.

Brick fences

Brick fences or walls are best used when the material is also featured elsewhere in the house; the matching materials create a design theme throughout your property. A well-crafted brick wall is a work of art that is best constructed by a professional. A bricklayer knows that although a short brick wall might be only 8 in. thick, the taller the wall, the thicker it must be for stability. Brick walls also need pillars installed at regular intervals for strength and stability.

OPPOSITE: Sustainably harvested Ipé, a wood from South America, can be an attractive choice for fence material.
ABOVE: A low brick wall topped with a row of potted geraniums, such as *Pelargonium* 'Vancouver Centennial', creates an attractive barrier.

The thickness, the pillars, and any decorative arrangements (such as pockets or openings) can serve as ornamentation in a brick wall. Adding a 12 to 18 in. trellis or several pots of flowers along the top of the wall increases the height of the barrier and creates more visual interest.

STONE

Low stone walls add weight to a landscape design, a solid presence surrounding the garden. Dry stack stone walls can stand without mortar—think of the miles of stone walls that line the farm fields of the American Northeast and run like ribbons across the fields of Ire-

land. Stone walls can line paths, follow corners or sidewalks, and act as barriers; the higher the wall, the more definite the statement.

Because most cities have codes restricting the height of fences and walls in the front of a property, low stone walls can be a good choice when you want to make a statement: a picket fence is sweet, but a stone wall carries some visual weight.

CONCRETE AND STUCCO

Gone are the days of boring, gray concrete expanses of patios or barriers around a property. Today's concrete walls have become artful barriers. Concrete can be tinted to resemble stone or stucco. It can be stamped with any design your heart desires—shells, leaves, or fish, for example. Use concrete to cover cinderblocks—when sprayed on, it takes on the look of stucco. (Granted, that idea would not be as stable as a wall created with formed, poured concrete.)

Concrete walls become a canvas to the garden artist: You can create mosaic designs with tumbled recycled glass, broken pottery, or tiles. Concrete walls can run straight along the property line or swirl around

OPPOSITE: Brick walls add a feeling of permanence to the landscape and can be used in a wide variety of styles, such as this formal design.
ABOVE, LEFT: A dry-stack stone wall provides nooks and crannies for tucked-in plants, including coral bells (*Heuchera sanguinea*).
ABOVE, RIGHT: Water spills down and along a channel carved in a low concrete wall that separates planting beds from the patio.

the landscape, and you can include pockets within the walls for fountains or planting along the way.

Create a wall of recycled concrete, such as pieces of busted up sidewalks, known nowadays as "urbanite." Recycled concrete is also useful for stepping-stones, and it can be fit together as a low dry-stack wall. Use recycled concrete for low retaining walls that keep a hillside from "trespassing" (sliding) into your garden.

Use stucco (a mixture of Portland cement, sand, and water) to cover formed concrete blocks. Use the blocks to build the wall, and spread the stucco over the blocks. Stucco can also be painted or decorated with glass, pottery, or tiles.

METAL AND COMBINATION BARRIERS

Metal barriers in the garden are no longer restricted to chain-link fences. Decorative metal fences offer a bit of flair; they look good and make effective barriers. But even if you use a chain-link fence as a barrier, it can be made beautiful, especially if you cover it with plants.

Wrought-iron fences are often painted black and convey a stately, sedate, and protective barrier, whether the fence is 3 ft. or 8 ft. high. This fence creates a traditional look that provides a heavyweight barrier with a light touch. Iron is a sturdy and solid material, but iron fences are usually formed in an open pattern that ranges from vertical pickets to curly filigree designs. Add some individuality by including finials on pickets and posts; choose a traditional motif, such as balls or pineapples on posts and arrows on pickets, or invent your own additions.

Other metals can be used in fencing as well. Copper tubing, for example, can be formed to create an interesting fencing effect. It will eventually lose its bright-and-shiny look as the metal develops a charming turquoise patina.

Create enclosures using galvanized steel panels; galvanized metal lasts a long time before it begins to rust. Or you might want it to rust: Rusted metal, used as a barrier, provides an organic look, as the rusted surfaces coordinate with the colors of leaves and flowers for an all-season appeal. Check online for steel architectural panels that can be used for fencing. Using products of various thicknesses and textures, you can create fences or ornaments.

Another unusual fencing material, hog wire, is no longer just for animals. Hog wire makes a good choice for a open garden fence and a perfect trellis material for climbing plants. The lightweight, high-strength, sometimes galvanized metal fencing alternative can be purchased in various heights and widths and comes in a roll or in long panels. Some types of hog wire must be stretched, and none of it is free-standing; you will need to attach panels to wooden or metal frames.

Even more options are available if you are looking for something unique. Gabion walls, for example, are constructed of two vertical panels of strong welded wire mesh that is filled with rocks, smooth stones, or recycled concrete. Gabion walls are rugged and inexpensive; they can be created in various shapes and styles. Ancient Romans built gabion fortresses (also called gabion baskets), and contemporary gabion walls are created by ranchers using stones removed from grazing pastures and highway departments looking for supporting or retaining wall structures. You can use this impressively strong display as a barrier in your landscape. Purchase premade gabion baskets or custom order the size you need. Tall barrier-style gabions should be securely installed with strong posts buried deep in the ground— the specifics depend on your particular project.

OPPOSITE, TOP LEFT: A chain-link fence need not be replaced. Instead, it can be decorated with a climbing rose, such as *Rosa* 'John Davis', and a purple-flowering clematis.
OPPOSITE, TOP RIGHT: An iron fence blends with the style of the home and landscape.
OPPOSITE, BOTTOM: Copper tubing bent into a series of arches provides an eye-catching barrier in this garden.

Natural materials

Plant material such as bamboo, willow, and reeds can be used to create an attractive wall or fence. The styles vary, but almost any fence made from plant material will add a rustic touch to your garden. Modern gardens sometimes include a rush or bamboo wall—a small surprise in a sea of clean lines and slim containers.

The sturdy culms (stalks) of bamboo can be used to create a long-lasting fence. Bamboo fencing is available in a variety of shapes, heights, rolls, and panels at many home and garden stores, or you make your own. To create a fence panel, bamboo culms are tied or wired together in lengths; install one panel or string several together. Depending on how they are made, bamboo fences can look rustic and casual or sophisticated and finished. In addition to the slender culms of bamboo, large-diameter timber bamboo cut into boards are used for a more finished project. Bamboo materials are often featured in Asian style gardens, but they can be suitable in a variety of landscape designs.

Rush fencing comprises sections of dried, thick grass attached vertically into a sort of thatch fence; it is usually sold in rolls. Because the material is flexible, it must be attached to intermittent posts, an existing fence, or some other support system or frame. Most rush fences are not durable enough to withstand years of inclement weather and will eventually decompose, so these fences are often considered temporary barriers.

To provide a low barrier, especially around your vegetable garden, interweave slender, flexible stems of willow, hazel, or other trees or shrubs to create a wattle fence. This ancient technique employs materials at hand, and the fences you create will be works of

art. Make a wattle fence yourself, find someone locally to create one for you, or buy a premade wattle fence from a garden store. Wattle fences are normally only a foot or two tall, but you can add a decorative wattle at the top of a trellis or to an existing fence to increase its height.

Composite products

Composite wood products may contain recycled wood or wood products and plastic (possibly recycled) or resin in varying percentages, depending on the brand you select. You will find composites for all sorts of outdoor structures, including fences, under brand names such as Trex and TimberTech. Composite materials are created to look similar to natural wood or stained wood, and they can be used exactly as lumber is used. They are long-lasting, durable, and require little or no maintenance.

OPPOSITE: An artistic gate with a carved heron shows the way to another part of the garden.
ABOVE, RIGHT: Well-designed bamboo fences make attractive barriers, and the material makes it easy for you to be creative with the design

THE GATED GARDEN

Even if you need to create a barrier around your garden, you—and others—also need a way to get in and out. A gate serves as a welcoming access portal or as a part of the barrier itself. If the lure of total seclusion beckons, and your front or back garden is sacrosanct, the gate leading into your garden must convey the need for exclusion, signaling that the proper "credentials" are required for entry. Of course, a solid gate—however secure it makes you feel—will not help you screen incoming visitors, unless you have installed a security camera as well.

If your gate looks too much like the fence, it can be virtually invisible, which will be a problem for invited guests, as they try to determine how to get in. The first courtesy you show visitors is a welcoming and well-marked entrance into your home. If the gate is difficult to locate along a long stretch of fence, visitors may wind up walking up and down the sidewalk before phoning you for directions.

To help mark a gate and make it an interesting part of the garden, add ornaments or accents, even something with a touch of humor. Consider adding an opening in the gate at eye level—an open circle, a fanciful moon, a sunflower, or a cat design. Make a tiny face-sized gate-within-a-gate, such as the one used by the bewhiskered Emerald City gatekeeper in *The Wizard of Oz*. Recycle materials by repurposing an old door or antique wrought iron grates from floor or wall registers or coal fireplaces for use as a decorative gate. Set within a wooden fence, a recycled gate shows off your creativity as well as its unique form.

OPPOSITE, TOP LEFT: A gate and pergola echo the home's architecture and pull together this small front garden design into a smart display. This structure also provides a solid barrier between the property and the sidewalk and street.
OPPOSITE, TOP RIGHT: The closed door of this gate implies a barrier, but when the top of the Dutch door is open, limited access and a view of the back garden are allowed.
OPPOSITE, BOTTOM: A well-designed, open-structured fence and gate barrier is surrounded by attractive plantings.

THE ILLUSION OF EXCLUSION

When a barbed-wire-topped, iron-clad, motion-detector-protected wall is overkill, an implied barrier might meet your needs. Sometimes a barrier simply suggests that access is limited. A velvet rope draped across the aisle at the theater does not stop us from walking through, but it does imply that we should stay outside that area until invited in. We also understand the meaning of a short, neatly clipped boxwood hedge placed around a vegetable or herb bed—it is not that we cannot cross the hedge, but we know we should not do so.

Semicircle designs deflect

Much as a pinball scoots around an inside curve and is shot back toward you, a C-shaped wall or hedge gives the impression that you need to stay on one side or the other. This barrier shape suggests limited access using the concept of deflection. The semicircle becomes an ornament that restricts movement beyond.

Even without including perimeter fencing, you can plant a semicircular garden on one side of your house to create a veritable boomerang effect. Instead of being led straight to the back of the house, visitors are captured in the curve before being sent back toward the sidewalk. In a sunny area, this deflective barrier could include a planting of azaleas—blowzy selections of *Rhododendron indica* that bloom in white or shades of pink in early spring. Other choices could include rock roses (*Cistus* spp.) or a short rhododendron selection such as 'Nancy Evans'. These shrubs rarely need more than a light pruning or shearing (just after flowering to preserve the next year's flowers).

Walk this way

BARRIERS WITHIN THE GARDEN

Using a barrier to enclose your garden or property is a solution to a particular problem, but even within your garden, you can direct visitors to walk only in certain areas or limit access to some areas to ensure privacy, to protect planted areas, or to allow visitors to experience your garden one "room" at a time. Use appropriate barriers within your garden to accomplish this.

Visitors might be able to see your front door from the driveway or the curb, but you can show them the best way into your home by designing structures and plantings that create a sense of purpose and provide a path. These elements serve as suggestive barriers that direct visitors where not to walk in your garden. Combine pathways through your property with barriers—some subtle, some less so—that mark the way into an entrance and create a feeling of order, no matter what the style of home and garden.

Establish a clear entrance to keep pedestrians on the path and discourage them from walking on lawns, beds, or other areas of your garden. Add an incentive by placing an archway or decorative fence posts over a path, even if no fence is attached, to mark the way. An archway at the beginning of a path from the sidewalk to the front door provides a subtle barrier, marking an entryway while making a stylish statement.

ABOVE: A low brick wall shaped in an semicircle creates the perfect place to display small pots and an evergreen clematis vine, while providing a barrier between the driveway and home entrance. A path behind the wall at the right leads to the driveway.
OPPOSITE: Tall, clipped hedges, a stone path, and solid, low-walled planters show visitors exactly where they should, and should not, walk in this garden.

Purpose is made even more plain when you place other subtle barriers along a path to encourage feet to stay on the walkway. Carve out sections of lawn to create pocket plantings of small trees, shrubs, and flowers around a path leading to different views and features of the garden.

Each path has a purpose in your garden, and the type of path you create conveys a message about its purpose. Use a wide path and shallow steps leading to the main entry to convey its intention. Narrow paths, especially winding paths, imply informality and a casual way to go.

Plant-lined beds placed on either side of a path create natural, subtle barriers. Adding a barrier of just a few inches on either side of the path encourages pedestrians to keep off the lawn or a special collection of primroses. In a woodland setting, planted beds outline a soft path of wood chips. In a more formal setting, maintain a clean line between path and garden bed by edging the path. A plethora of possibilities exist for edging a path, including natural woody material such as hoops of red-twig dogwood (*Cornus sericea*) or willow (*Salix* spp.), both of which will readily sprout and root to form a fluffy edge and eventually a small barrier hedge that will need to be clipped.

Use other materials, such as concrete scallops, bricks set upright, or even wine bottles buried topside down, to line a path. Line a path with stone-walled planters; when paired with stone or crushed rock pathways, they provide barriers that help guide pedestrians' feet. On terraced or sloped land, create a sunken path surrounded by tall, stone-sided, planted barriers that create a sense of privacy.

OPPOSITE, TOP: A low rock wall and an assortment of plants serve as barriers when situated on both sides of a entry sidewalk, showing visitors where to walk and where not to walk.
OPPOSITE, BOTTOM LEFT: Defined flagstone paths lead the way to the front door and to the side of the house. Surrounding plantings serve as subtle barriers that discourage pedestrians from walking off the path.
OPPOSITE, BOTTOM RIGHT: Stone walls hold soil in raised beds along a sunken path leading to the back side of a house.

Parterres and knot gardens

A parterre is a formal garden of planted herbs and flowers arranged in a decorative way, usually in geometric shapes lined by low clipped hedges or low stone walls. A knot garden is a type of parterre, with clipped plants such as thyme and germander pruned to appear as though they are woven into a pattern over and under each other. Parterres are often best viewed from a distance, especially from a window above, where you can appreciate the garden's geometric patterns. The parterre style became popular in the sixteenth century and is still used in gardens today.

Low parterre hedges can be used to discourage people and animals from walking through the plantings of annuals or vegetables. The small evergreen shrubs most commonly used as barriers in a parterre include boxwood (*Buxus* spp.), Japanese holly (*Ilex crenata*, especially 'Convexa' and 'Helleri'), and other low-growing plants such as dwarf yaupon holly (*I. vomitoria* 'Stokes Dwarf'). Parterres and knot gardens create a kind of privacy in your garden—on a small scale.

ABOVE, LEFT: A parterre of tightly clipped boxwood creates geometric spaces into which annual flowers and vegetables are planted and displayed to fine effect.

ABOVE, RIGHT: Parterres can be created using many whimsical shapes, including curlicues.

ABOVE: Parterres and knot gardens can be arranged in a variety of decorative motifs.

WILDLIFE BARRIERS

No garden can be devoid of living creatures, but for many gardeners, some creatures, such as deer, rabbits, raccoons, and other people's dogs and cats, eat and trample plants or otherwise disrupt the garden. Unwanted wildlife and pet trespassers can be a constant headache—deer eating the roses, raccoons stripping the corn, or the cat next door using the flowerbed as a litter box. We do not want to hurt them, but we want them to stay out of our gardens.

BELOW: An artfully designed double fence, each 5 ft. high, with a 5 ft. space between, keeps deer from jumping into the vegetable garden and also provides a attractive trellis for climbing plants.

Deer

When it comes to deer, everybody has a favorite remedy—from hanging bars of soap or bags of animal waste in the trees, to spraying leaves with smelly liquids (that must be reapplied continually), to using motion-activated sprinklers that soak the gardener as often as the deer. Restrictive plant lists may work for some, but many gardeners are tired of asking "Will deer eat it?" or trying to second-guess the animals' likes and dislikes, which change from season to season. At the bottom of almost every list of plants that "deer won't eat" is a caveat: "They will eat anything if they are sufficiently hungry."

Motion-sensors that set off a sharp spray from the sprinkler can deter deer and other marauding animals—but you need to remember to turn off the sensor before you head outside to fetch the morning paper.

Other gardeners find that they must move the sprinkler around the garden regularly, or else the deer become accustomed to where they will, and will not, get sprayed.

Barriers are the key to excluding deer from the garden. You can protect individual trees and shrubs, when young, by surrounding the plant with a wire cage. Loosely wrap woven wire fences around the trunks of young trees until the tree is established. As the tree grows, it can sustain some browsing damage, although deer will stand on their back feet to reach up into an apple tree and browse on fruit and leaves.

If you are protecting an entire orchard, consider using a fence barrier. A deer fence may not seem feasible—you might think it will be unattractive, that fencing the entire area is impossible, or that your yard will look like a prison. But many examples of successful deer fences in beautiful gardens exist to alleviate those fears.

The necessary height of the fence—one that jumping deer cannot clear—depends on the type of deer in your neighborhood. White-tailed deer may not jump a 6 ft. fence, but mule deer will. Deer are less likely to jump a solid fence, because they cannot see through to the other side. Deer are also less likely to jump a double fence. Surround your most important plants—whether they be vegetables or roses—with two 5 ft. fences with a 5 ft. space between them. You can use hog wire and sturdy 4-by-4 posts. Use the inner fence as a trellis for climbing beans, peas, or flowers such as nasturtiums or sweet peas. The 5 ft. space between the two fences will accommodate more plants or a pathway.

Even if you build an effective barrier to keep deer out of the garden, conceding some garden space to the deer can mean, first, that you are not constantly annoyed, and, second, that the deer will be preoccupied with what they *can* eat, not what they cannot eat.

Rabbits

To keep rabbits from digging under or hopping over a fence, bury 1 ft. of a 3 ft. tall wire fence in the ground. The fencing should have openings no bigger than an inch. You can attach wire rabbit fencing to the inside of an ornamental fence and it will be hidden, at least partially, from view. Use tree guards made from wire mesh or fencing to protect individual trees and shrubs from hungry rabbits. Fan out the wire onto the ground and make sure it covers at least 2 ft. up the trunk.

Raccoons

Raccoons can be fenced out of your corn patch by installing a floppy wire fence—they need a sturdy structure on which to climb. Install the fence in a C-shape, and secure the bottom of the fence to the ground. Prevent raccoons from climbing up fruit trees or grape trellises by installing a predator guard—wrap a 24 in. wide piece of galvanized vent pipe around the trunk;

this will make it too slippery to climb. Or form a funnel out of galvanized sheet metal by snipping and bending, so that the flare points down and extends at least 18 in. from the trunk. Attach the funnel to the tree with short nails or tacks.

Squirrels

Many gardeners distract squirrels from bird feeders or fruit trees by giving them their own stash of peanuts, presented in some puzzling way that takes the squirrel at least a few minutes to figure out. You can use predator guards similar to those used for raccoons to keep squirrels out of trees. Squirrels are good jumpers; if branches of a tree, the top of a fence, or the edge of a roof is anywhere within range, they will use it as a launch pad.

If you want to keep squirrels out of a bird feeder, try hanging the feeder on a slick pole away from jumping points. Some bird feeders use a grated covering with holes that allow birds to feed at the seed ports; a squirrel's weight triggers the grated covering to slip down so that the ports are misaligned with the openings and the squirrel cannot feed.

Squirrels love to dig in loose, freshly dug soil. They will also dig up and eat tulip and crocus bulbs, and although they will not eat daffodil or ornamental onion bulbs (*Allium* spp.), they will dig them up. After planting bulbs, cover the area with hardware cloth—wire cloth with 1/4 in. openings—or plant bulbs in underground wire boxes purchased from a bulb catalog or garden store.

The easiest way to keep the squirrels from digging into soil is to water well after planting—saturate the soil. Squirrels prefer not to dig in wet soil, and by the time the soil has started to dry out, the smell of the bulbs is diminished.

Birds and fruit trees

Bird netting keeps birds out of fruit trees, so that you get the fruit before they do. Whether your garden includes individual miniature dwarf trees or just a few blueberry bushes, consider using a pop-up netted box made from all-weather polypropylene or another long-lasting material. Just like a pop-up tent, the netted boxes are easy to set in place; set them up before fruit starts to ripen. Pop-up netted boxes come in various sizes, and you can find short boxes for vegetable beds (to keep crows from pulling up seedlings), to boxes up to 4 ft. high.

Dwarf, miniature dwarf, and espaliered fruit trees—highly productive choices for the city garden—are easy to cover with bird netting, which is usually made of black plastic, with 1/2 in. holes. Most bird netting is folded up, in sizes up to 100 ft. long, which can be unwieldy to unfold and put in place. You and a helper can secure the netting over the plant and tie it in place at the base, leaving no large holes; otherwise, you can trap birds inside, instead of keeping them out.

If you grow much shrub fruit, such as blueberries, currants, and blackberries, and you have a miniature orchard in your backyard, consider creating a walk-in cage of wire mesh to keep your fruit safe from marauding animals.

Cats and dogs

Do not blame the cat—all it sees is a wide expanse of bare soil. Instead of creating a neighborhood litter box, design your garden with layers of plants that act as a barrier. Cats do not like to walk on uneven ground, so create garden plots that are as uneven as possible. In open areas, lay out slightly crunched-up pieces of chicken wire, lay sticks in a crosswise fashion, or use odds and ends of lattice as deterrents. Some cat-deterring materials use plastic "spikes" (that will not injure you or the cat): Place pieces of the material in the garden where you do not want cats to walk or dig. These products come in shades of brown plastic that fades into the color of the ground. Cat deterrents help the local bird population, too. Indoor-only cats lead long and happy lives: consider keeping your cat inside.

Many city ordinances require that dog owners keep their pets on a leash and/or inside a fenced area; owners are also required to clean up after their dogs. In a perfect world, your garden, your lawn, and your chickens would be safe from dogs, but such is not always the case in the real world. Fences and walls will keep dogs out, and a vast array of products—ranging from garlic, to red pepper, to peppermint oil—is available to help repel dogs (and cats and squirrels) from particular areas.

SCREENS

Solutions for Unwanted Sights

On lots large and small, from estates to condos, homeowners seeking a little privacy or relief from unwanted views—from unsightly garbage bins, to the neighbor's hot tub—react by reaching for massive, monotonous hedges or the tallest fence possible. We need privacy—a way to hide or disguise unwanted views or a place to rest without being viewed by others—but grand "solutions" are overkill.

A screen fulfills its role in the garden by obstructing a view inside or outside the garden. Often, the things you want to hide are the necessities of modern living.

- Ugly garbage and recycling bins are in full view of your patio.
- Lawn mower, leaf blower, edger—all that lawn equipment needs a hiding place.
- You need a potting bench and compost bin—but you do not need to see them every time you look out your window.
- The water meter and air-conditioning unit are ugly intrusions in your garden.
- You need to install a screen along a path at the side of your house, but only 10 ft. of space is available.
- The neighbor's living room window offers a clear view of your patio; you want to block the view from that one window.
- You want to add height to your fence, but city ordinances limit how tall it can be built.
- People walking by can see into your garden, and you need a screen to block eye-level views.
- The big, blank garage wall fills the view from your kitchen window.
- A hedge is the best type of screening solution for you, but what type of hedge should you plant, and how will you maintain it?
- You have no garden soil in which to add plants, but you want to create a screen using plants in containers.

Screens should add to the overall design and interest in your garden. As a visual design element, a screen adds texture, structure, height, and form. The best screen hides the garbage bin but offers visual interest as well. Consider both the function—to hide or distract—as well as the ornamental benefits of screening, and take advantage of the opportunity to improve how your garden looks and feels, instead of concentrating on a single aspect.

THE SCREEN WITHIN
Screening Areas Inside Your Property

Imagine a backdoor view of a small suburban or urban garden. All the components required to accommodate relaxing and entertaining are present: the patio, table, and chairs—along with the air conditioner unit, garbage can, recycling bin, and compost pile. Functional parts of the landscape—including immoveable items such as the air conditioner—need to be accessible, yet they should not be focal points. Creative screening can help you hide an eyesore; use a disguise to conceal the necessary from plain sight, and none will be the wiser.

As you devise solutions to disguise or screen off parts of your outdoor life, remember that your property has much more to offer than you might realize. Even the smallest lots and tiniest urban gardens are loaded with nifty spots that offer a place to sit, a place to dig, a place to grow your favorite plants, and a place to hide bins, compost piles, and other distractions. Even in small gardens, unused corners or side yards can serve as places to store eyesores. Consider the side of the garage or a side of your house seldom viewed.

Keep two important factors in mind when placing bins and other necessary tools out of site: your accessibility to the bins and your neighbors' view of them. Accessibility should be paramount—you want to avoid a tangle with a thorny shrub planted too near the area surrounding bins, and the bins should not be placed too far from the door. But equally important is the view of the eyesore—both yours and your neighbors. Rather than stash the bins in a convenient spot where your neighbors can see them, consider a place beyond everyone's view. You do not want to see these eyesores, and neither do the neighbors.

PREVIOUS PAGE: Fence panels are set in a staggered pattern to provide a screen, rather than a barrier, between the house and the sidewalk.
OPPOSITE, LEFT AND RIGHT: A brick wall and fountain within the garden, at left, hide a utility-access path that runs along the back fence of the garden, at right.

Screening garbage and recycling bins

Instead of installing a prefab tool shed to store garden tools and household bins, you can design and build a simple corral for these items that serves aesthetically as part of the garden. And rounding up your household bins saves you time by creating a one-stop storage place.

Install a three-sided corral against your house or garage using prebuilt lattice panels that you can purchase in framed or ready-to-frame styles. Attach the panels to in-ground posts, and install a wide-swinging gate on one side, with plenty of room for maneuvering the bins. Paint, stain, or leave the wooden lattice unadorned, just as you would a fence. Keep the floor of the corral clean and level by using pavers set in sand framed in sturdy pieces of lumber, so that you can open and close the gate and roll bins in and out without fighting uneven ground.

If garbage and yard waste bin collections occur at the street, build a corral against an existing fence at the front of your property to hide the bins closer to the pickup spot. You can create a smooth and well-hidden—

yet still accessible—screen by building a bin corral in the same style as the fence next to it; it will fade into the existing fencing instead of calling attention to itself.

Look around for unused and useful space. An area under a porch or deck, for example, can become a hidden storage area of sufficient height and width to accommodate bins that need be hauled in and out only occasionally. Create a more finished look by framing in and enclosing the space using lattice panels or a custom-designed fence that is hinged to swing open as a gate.

ABOVE, LEFT: Stored out of sight in a stylish corral, garbage and recycling bins await collection day.
ABOVE, RIGHT: A modern metal sculpture that functions as a swivel gate hides the neighbor's garbage bins stored at the side of the house. The metal artist was Lance Carelton.

Using screens to hide large equipment

Store an array of large garden tools behind an attractive screen to keep them organized and accessible. Garages are, of course, a garden tool storage option, but garages are best used to store other things—boxes of high school mementos, Christmas decorations, old toys, woodworking equipment, new bathroom fixtures yet to be installed, and perhaps even a car or two. Unsightly but necessary items may be hidden from view, but they should not be difficult to access and use. Instead of hauling garden tools from one end of your property to another, look for alternative storage options that keep tools close at hand and that suit your style and your lifestyle.

ABOVE, LEFT AND RIGHT: Screening panels built against a matching fence are hardly noticeable as they enclose and hide garbage and recycling bins.

Large items can be hidden behind a false wall, similar to the theatrical device that uses a short wall erected downstage (that is, closer to the audience than the actual back wall of a set). The false wall gives the actors a place to move off stage and out of a scene. Instead of hiding actors, you can hide all sorts of garden implements behind a false wall erected in a corner of the garden or along a permanent wall, providing a narrow storage area. Create a false wall using a variety of materials, such as a concrete block covered with tinted stucco.

Under the generous porches of old houses are crawl spaces that are often just dark holes. Conceal the unpleasant, cavelike space underneath a high deck or porch by securing lattice or other fencing material as a screen, perhaps adding a vine to contribute vertical interest and connect the deck to the garden below. Or, instead of permanently attaching panels to cover the space, install a hinged panel and use the space underneath the porch for storage. Even if you choose not to use the crawl space for storage, at least the "black hole" will be hidden. Plants and shrubs, especially those with variegated leaves or colorful flowers, can also be used as effective screens to hide the dark area under the porch.

If you choose not to build a structure, you might discover another secret place to stash a lawnmower, a shovel, or a small cart—under a tree, perhaps. Evergreens with low branches can provide convenient hiding places; you will know what is stored beneath those branches, but nobody else would suspect that a lovely skirt of foliage is hiding garden equipment.

Work areas

Empty containers, pots of expired tulips, bags of potting soil, stakes for the dahlias, and more can pile up around your potting bench. A view of a work area reminds you of all those unfinished garden tasks. If you have the space, you probably have a working compost bin or pile. Although it feels good to create fresh compost to add to your garden, you might wish that you could avoid the view of that pile of yard waste or black plastic contraption every time you sit outside with a cup of coffee—sometimes, you just want to relax and enjoy the view. Create a screen to hide a work area or compost bin by planting a short length of hedge that is low enough to keep the perimeter of your garden and other views in sight, while hiding a compost or work area and all that entails. Choose an evergreen hedge for a year-round screen.

Solve both unattractive issues by incorporating a bit of the working garden into a screen. A compost fence includes twigs, leaves, bits of branches, and spent flowers that decompose in a narrow space between two lengths of hog wire. The various shades of

Accessing bins under a porch or deck

You can provide easy access to garbage and recycling or compost bins stored under a raised porch or deck by creating bench seats that open to reveal the bins below. The benches double as bin access, so that you need only lift up the bench seat and drop the items into the open bin. After guests finish their barbecue, encourage them to stand up, lift the bench lids, and drop their compostable plates and recyclable plates into the appropriate bins in this modified chute system. On pickup day, walk down the steps to ground level, open the gate to the space under the deck, pull out the bins, and take them to the curb. Under-seat storage can also be used for tools, and the bench you sit upon to drink your morning coffee could hide the worm bin that awaits your coffee grounds.

brown and the textures of leaf and stem combine to create a visually pleasing—and unusual—fence to set off and conceal a part of your garden. Compost fences are an ingenious way to keep your garden trimmings onsite and let them decompose naturally, while providing a screen that is both functional and attractive.

OPPOSITE: Benches on a small back porch can double as access to garbage and recycling bins below. On collection day, the gates are opened at ground level and bins are wheeled to the curb.

Create a compost fence using two panels of heavy-gauge hog wire fencing that are extended between posts, with a 4 to 6 in. space between the two panels. The actual width of the space is determined by the size of post you use (a 4-by-4 post would create a 4 in. wide space, for example). Place compostable yard waste items into the long, narrow opening between the two fence panels. The material can be compacted using the handle end of a shovel or another narrow implement. It may not look like much when you begin, but as you add trimmings, pruned stems, grass clippings, and spent flowers to the compost fence, the level of the contents will rise, creating a tapestry wall of plant material.

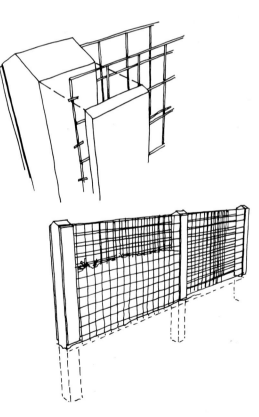

OPPOSITE: A blue stucco wall creates an attractive screen. Behind the wooden door, a lawnmower and other garden tools are stored out of sight.

ABOVE, LEFT: Brightly colored shrubs serve as a screen that lightens the dark space under a porch.

ABOVE, RIGHT: A compost fence serves as both form and function in the garden: It disguises the work area, provides a backdrop for plantings at its base, and stores compostable material on site.

RIGHT: Create a compost fence between two lengths of hog wire fence secured onto posts and then filled with clippings and prunings.

As the yard waste at the bottom layer in the fence breaks down, the space at the top becomes available for adding more. A narrow planting bed at the base of the fence can catch and use the bits of finished compost as it drops down.

Two notes of caution are warranted regarding compost walls: Avoid adding tenacious weeds to the wall. If you do include weeds, chop or break them apart, and do not include their roots, flowers, or seed heads, or the plants will grow in the wall. And, as interesting as it might look, banana peels and other food scraps added to the wall can attract rodents, so they should also be avoided.

Hiding large, boxy utility items

An air conditioner unit or utility meter need not be an eyesore in the middle of your barbecue area. Both bulky and stationary, air conditioner units and utility meters should be accessible but should not be center stage in a garden. If you have space to spare, plant shrubs and tall perennials around these ugly features to hide them. Provide a discreet path around a planted screen—a few stepping stones, a patch of crushed rock—to remind you to prune back the shrubs and to show utility workers and others where to access the equipment.

If you have no in-ground space available for planting—if the eyesores are surrounded by a patio, for example—install a bit of free-standing green by creating a living wall. Living walls are vertical gardens that can include all manner of plants, from ferns, to succulents, to vegetables. Living walls, built on frames, use rows or individual cells or feltlike grow bags that hold a bit of growing medium and plants. A drip system installed at the top of the wall or running horizontally along several sections uses a surprisingly small amount of water to sustain the plants.

Screening blank spaces

Use a screen to cover large, boring surfaces and blank spaces within your garden, such as monotonous fences and windowless garage walls. Planted in front of a bare wall, shrubs, vines, and other plants can serve as

a screen that creates visual interest. Shrubs and vines can be trained against or secured onto a wall or fence, espaliered or pruned so that they lie flat against the surface. Espaliered plants can be grown in a variety of styles and shapes, including fan and candelabra shapes, or as a Belgian fence, a diamond-patterned espalier form. Or use espaliered plants to form a free-standing living screen.

ABOVE: Hide an air conditioning unit behind shrubbery, but remember, as shown in this plan view, that you will need access to the unit, and include some clearance so that the unit can function properly.
OPPOSITE, TOP: A short lattice fence panel and billowing hydrangeas hide an air conditioning unit behind bright flowers and foliage.
OPPOSITE, BOTTOM: A poodle-clipped *Euonymus kiautschovicus* 'Manhattan' and hanging pots of geraniums with bright pink blossoms offer interesting visual textures against a weathered fence.

Using illusion

"Pay no attention to that man behind the curtain!" the Wizard of Oz says to Dorothy. And many homeowners would like to express similar sentiments: Pay no attention to the neighbor's ugly wall at the back of my garden. Without resorting to wizardry, you can create illusions in your garden to soften unwanted views and create the appearance of more space.

During the fifteenth century, artists used trompe l'oeil techniques to create realistic paintings and frescoes on walls and ceilings. Trompe l'oeil uses perspective to fool the viewer's eye into seeing three dimensions instead of two. It can be used in today's garden as well as in the art gallery. A trompe l'oeil painting on a flat, boring wall can provide the illusion, through perspective, of more room in the garden.

Instead of painting a wall, erect a trellis or archway designed to create a false perspective against a wall. Successively smaller interior rings of trellis make the structure appear to expand farther and farther away. Trellises without the built-in false perspective still provide good screening for a blank wall (leave a few inches between trellis and wall to ensure air circulation and allow for maintenance). In addition, because an arch or trellis need not be mounted onto a surface, you can use it to disguise a blank neighboring wall by placing it just inside your property line. Plant vines to weave in and out of the structure to combine the false perspective with real greenery.

ABOVE, RIGHT: A thoughtfully placed three-paneled mirror window acts as a screen and provides the illusion of more space in a small garden.
OPPOSITE, TOP: The addition of a lattice and plants at the corner of a property screens the view of the busy street.

Fruit trees display their flowers and fruit well when trained as espaliers. And because the trees are grown in a compact, two-dimensional fashion, fruit is easy to harvest. Grape vines and figs can also be espaliered, as well as ornamental plants, such as firethorn (*Pyracantha*), flowering quince (*Chaenomeles*), camellias such as *Camellia sasanqua*, and many selections of viburnum.

Even if they are not trained into an espalier or other form, shrubs planted close to a wall need to be pruned so that they do not outgrow the space. Selectively prune branches that extend too far into a path or that shoot up and over the roof line. Old-fashioned rambling roses make excellent wall shrubs that need regular pruning; left to their own devices, they will out-

grow the space. With short branches trained horizontally, a rambling rose grown in full sun will bloom profusely, adding beauty to a plain wall. Considering the following roses for their attractive and fragrant flowers: white and fragrant *Rosa* 'Adélaide d'Orléans'; pink and white, double-flowered *R.* 'Félicité Perpétue'; or fragrant, pink, double-flowered *R.* 'Paul's Himalayan Musk'.

Vines will also cover an unsightly wall surface. Some vines are self-attaching and can adhere to a vertical surface, such as creeping fig (*Ficus pumila*), Boston ivy (*Parthenocissus tricuspidata*), and silvervein creeper vine (*P. henryana*). Climbing hydrangea, *Hydrangea anomala* subsp. *petiolaris*, grows short roots that cling to surfaces. Other vines need support, such as twining plants. If you are using vines or plants to cover a brick

wall, attach wires or other support structures using masonry nails. For a wood structure, install eye-bolts and wires for support.

In cool or cold-winter regions, take advantage of the extra warmth and reflected light of a wall surface and plant a shrub or vine that is considered marginally hardy in your zone. For example, many California lilac (*Ceanothus*) selections, hardy to Zone 8, can be grown against a protected wall in Zone 7. A flowering maple, such as *Abutilon vitifolium*, hardy to Zone 10, could be planted next to a sunny wall in the maritime Pacific Northwest, Zones 8–9, with protection. Citrus, hardy in southern coastal and inland regions of the United States, can be planted against a sun-facing wall; although the plants will suffer damage in particularly cold winters, they offer the possibility of fresh-squeezed orange juice. On the other hand, be careful that plants do not can bake in too much heat when planted against a sun-reflecting wall.

In cold-weather regions, a protected, warm area may become a problem in itself. When temperatures are below freezing, hardy woody plants slow down their physiological processes; when sunlight hits the bark or stem of the plant, it can warm the tissue enough so that it expands, only to freeze again at nightfall. This can cause sunscald—dieback—and can damage foliage as well.

SCREENING OUT
Hiding, Covering, and Disguising Unwanted Views Outside the Garden

It can be easy to generalize screening needs and overcompensate by erecting a 30 ft. long Leyland cypress or arborvitae hedge to hide an unwanted view. But such drastic measures are not usually necessary and often end up creating more of a problem than a solution. Good screens disguise and divert; they do not barricade.

Screening possibilities for narrow spaces may not be abundant, but they do exist. If, for example, you want to screen a view into your next-door neighbor's bedroom window, erect a selective screen to cover only the view of the window, instead of erecting a large hedge that blocks your view of the majestic oaks growing in the park a few doors down. Or add a few inches to an existing fence—easier than erecting a new structure or planting a hedge. Plant an eye-level screen, and leave room for flowers or vegetables at the ground level.

Screens for narrow places

In urban and suburban neighborhoods, homes are often built on small lots with only narrow spaces between them in which to travel from front to back. A functional space with a path may not require a full screen, unless the neighbor's nearby windows make you feel like you are being watched every time you walk there.

Narrow space screening requires special attention, because one wrong plant selection can mean you pay for it with continual maintenance and ongoing headaches—for example, keeping a sprawling spirea pruned to fit a tiny space would be a constant chore. Look for trees and shrubs that fit the planting area instead of trying to squeeze a large plant into a tight space. Think creatively as you choose plants: A mix of plants works just as well as a long line of a single type of plant. A few tall, thin plants combined with a vine-covered trellis might do the trick.

Carefully positioned trees, chosen for their mature height or spread, make effective screens in narrow spaces. A small tree, a series of small trees or limbed-up (pruned to standard) large shrubs, or a grouping of artfully placed small trees can serve as effective screens.

OPPOSITE, TOP LEFT: A limbed-up crape myrtle (*Lagerstroemia*) provides an eye-level screen between adjoining properties, with available planting space around its base.
OPPOSITE, TOP RIGHT: Narrow plants such as Italian cypress (*Cupressus sempervirens*) and a clipped hedge can be used in tight spaces to provide a privacy screen along a walkway between two properties.

Selective screening

Close quarters are a part of daily living in cities and suburbs, and although most city dwellers do not mind being a bit up close and personal with their neighbors, everyone draws the line somewhere. Window-to-window screening is mandatory if you look out your window to a view inside your neighbor's house, or if, for example, a path between your house and the neighbor's house passes by a low window in your home. You might not need a screen for the entire length of the path, but you want to spot screen the area between the path and your window.

You can selectively screen an area without resorting to a fence or long row of shrubs. Before you plant, consider the environment and other factors to choose the best screening plant for the job. A short screen to deflect peering eyes (yours or theirs) helps retain a sense of privacy. Narrow junipers and pencil-thin Italian cypress may come to mind as a first solution, but they are sun-loving plants, and often narrow spaces are shaded by the very houses that need the privacy. A few narrow-growing, shade-tolerant plants can be used as spot screens, however. *Buxus* 'Monrue' (Green Tower boxwood) and *B. sempervirens* 'Graham Blandy'

tolerate some shade and can grow to 9 ft. tall with a 2 ft. spread. *Nandina domestica* (heavenly bamboo), to 5 ft., grows well in shade. If the offending window is on the second story, sufficient sun might be available to sustain a sun-loving tree. The tops of a small, well-placed *Taxus ×media* 'Hicksii' (Hick's yew, 20 × 6 ft.) or *Sciadopitys verticillata* 'Joe Kozey' (Japanese umbrella pine, 10 × 2 ft.) can get the light it needs.

To begin analyzing a situation for choosing the best screening option, enlist the help of a friend or family member. If a neighbor's window overlooks your patio, have a seat at the table or in your Adirondack chair on the patio, and ask your friend to walk across the particular part of the property that needs screening. When you friend arrives at a problematic spot, mark it in some way.

Check sightlines, and then estimate the required height of the spot screen by considering the height of most homes' features. Usually, for example, in a one-story house, the height from foundation to gutters is about 10 ft. If you need to screen a window on the ground floor, a 5 to 10 ft. tall shrub or dwarf tree will probably do the trick; if the window is on the second floor, you will need to plant a tree that grows to about 15 ft. or taller.

OPPOSITE, TOP: A narrow screen of deciduous trees allows in plenty of light for bulbs planted beneath.
OPPOSITE, BOTTOM LEFT: A trellis covered in Boston ivy (*Parthenocissus tricuspidata*) provides spot screening as well as seasonal color.
OPPOSITE, BOTTOM RIGHT: Small trees, such as variegated giant dogwood (*Cornus controversa* 'Variegata'), planted between a property and the roadway can provide screening, but if the vegetation is too dense, it can block drivers' and pedestrians' views, creating a safety hazard.

Sightlines matter

Large, bulky plants placed at street corners or within planting strips between a property and the street can block drivers' and pedestrians' views. You may think that a tall conifer provides a good anchor at the corner of your property, but if that corner is also an important sightline for drivers, the conifer is creating a potentially dangerous situation.

The planting strip between sidewalk and street might be owned by the city, and although you plant a garden there, the area is ultimately the city's responsibility. More gardeners are taking to the curbside to plant small shrubs, perennials, and ground covers. As strip planting increases, so should our awareness of what makes the streets safe for drivers, pedestrians, children, and pets.

Many municipalities have created restrictions on planting and structure heights along roadways, so you should remember some general guidelines as you plan your planting stip. Plants at street corners should be no taller than 2 ft., and plants within a planting strip should be no taller than 3 ft. Street trees are not an exception, but they are a different category altogether. The space that the trunk occupies between ground and canopy provides the necessary sightlines, and regulations often require that street tree canopies be high enough not to impede pedestrians on the sidewalk or vehicles on the street. Conifers can be problematic, however, because their branches usually extend all the way to the ground, and they can block the views of both drivers and pedestrians.

Using trellises as screens

The ultimate in a thin screen may well be a trellis. Sometimes a freestanding trellis alone provides a sufficient screen, or you can add some greenery by choosing plants to decorate it. Attach a trellis to the top of a fence that runs between properties, and plant vining or climbing plants to weave through it. You can find trellises in a variety of materials. Wooden fence-top lattice panels are easy to come by at many hardware and lumber stores, but you can use other materials as well. A metal trellis made of rebar, hog wire, or wire mesh provides the perfect structure for supporting twining vines.

Choose vines and twining plants that are appropriate for the space (shade-tolerant or sun-loving, for example), and know their growth habits so that you can avoid spending too much time tying up vines and pinning them back. Twining plants include black-eyed Susan vine (*Thunbergia alata*) and many varieties of clematis, which twist their petioles or stems around a support. Sweet peas (*Lathyrus* spp.) use tendrils to attach.

Using distraction as a screen

Use eye-catching distractions to draw a visitor's eyes to a feature instead of an eyesore. Distractions show them what you want them to see, not what you want to hide—just as a magician draws your eye to what he wants you to see, so that you miss his sleight-of-hand. If, for example, a view of the neighbor's motor home or shop area is visible as you and your guests walk onto your backyard patio area, place a water feature near the patio to draw attention away from the eyesore and away from the direct line of sight. The sound of a fountain or waterfall will attract visitors' attention. Water is magic in the garden—eyes will seek the source of the sound and the unwanted view will go unnoticed. Water masks sound and attracts the eye; add those benefits to its list of good qualities.

Fence height restrictions

Although restrictions vary by housing association, city, and county, the usual height restriction for fences is 6 ft. The restriction could be 5 ft. where you live, or 6 ft. at the rear of your property and 3 or 4 ft. in front, and setback restrictions for front fences may apply as well. Adding a 2 ft. trellis or arbor atop a 6 ft. fence may be allowed, depending on local ordinances. Always check with your local government before spending the time and money to install a fence or trellis to avoid having to modify it or tear it down if it does not meet restrictions.

Use a garden feature or attractive planting not only to draw the eye away from something, but to call attention to something else. Perhaps a particularly fetching tree, lovely in all seasons, is visible in your neighbor's garden. Make the most of a "borrowed view" of the neighbor's tree by placing a water feature or other attractive element in your garden in a way that leads the eye from the feature to the tree. Stand in your garden and look around to see what landscape characteristics you might borrow from nearby properties—be it an old church bell tower or a large flowering dogwood two doors down. Then select and place a garden feature within the sightline of that view.

OPPOSITE, TOP LEFT: A trellis surrounded by attractive vines, trees, and perennials provides a thin screen that allows light to pass through.
OPPOSITE, TOP RIGHT: A climbing rose arches up and over the lattice top of a fence, adding height and more privacy to the screen between backyard gardens.
OPPOSITE, BOTTOM: A water feature in the garden provides an aural distraction and draws the eye away from unpleasant views.

You can also use a "scatter-screen" approach to distract from an unwanted view or lead the eye to a better view. Instead of a planting a solid hedge, plant the same type of shrub or tree in random arrangements of three to five plants to attract attention to the plant groupings instead of what lies beyond, even without entirely blocking the view.

Scrims: A light covering screen

In the theater, a scrim is created using a gauzy material to hide one set from the audience while a scene is being played on another set. The scrim is often painted; when lighted, it becomes a wall, and when lit from behind, the scrim becomes an ethereal screen. Plants and garden structures, like a scrim, can be used to provide a soft visual illusion of a screen. Small-leaved plants, for example, provide just enough texture to screen what lies beyond.

The evergreen boxleaf azara (*Azara microphylla*) creates an excellent green scrim; with its tiny leaves and a mature height of about 15 ft., two or three plants can form a haze of green (or green and white, with cultivar 'Variegata'). In colder climates, create a scrim from the deciduous, small-leaved Siberian peashrub (*Caragana arborescens*).

A few selections of plants with weeping, or fountain, shapes can be trained to create a curtain between you and your neighbor in a narrow space. The weeping blue atlas cedar (*Cedrus atlantica* 'Glauca Pendula'), for example, grows as tall as it is staked, but it will reach 40 ft. tall or long, depending on how you train it. If the tree is trained up a stake and then along a fence line, its weeping branches fall toward the ground, forming a blue-hazed scrim. The Serbian spruce (*Picea omorika* 'Pendula') grows in the same fashion.

Search nurseries for plants that are already the height you want, or buy a young tree with a weeping form and flexible new stems (instead of a mature, woody trunk) to train. Horizontal branches might need to be supported, much as you would a fruit tree espalier. Eventually, the horizontal branches of a weeping tree will grow stronger, although they will need occasional support along the length of the plant.

THE HEDGE SOLUTION

Today's urban and suburban hedges serve to enclose a space, while providing a living screen that contributes to the garden's verdancy. A light hedge might be the best solution for preventing people from looking into your property or for hiding unpleasant views outside the garden. Perhaps a light hedge around the hot tub will keep neighbors from gawking, or the hedge screen that runs the width of your backyard will lessen the imposition of the golf course beyond.

ABOVE, LEFT: A trellis fence and a boxleaf azara (*Azara microphylla*) work together to provide a scrim.
ABOVE, RIGHT: A wall of water forms an effective scrim between a side garden and the back patio.

Before planting, do a little research to determine which plants, what styles, what places, and how best to grow and maintain a hedge. A well-chosen, planted, and maintained hedge will screen off the neighbor's driveway, cover a chain-link fence, or hide the convenience store sign at the corner. An improperly chosen, planted, or maintained hedge is a nightmare of dead and dying eyesores that encroach on your and your neighbor's spaces.

Hedge screening offers a few advantages over metal or wooden counterparts. Fence maintenance—at least the wooden kind—includes painting, staining, and replacing panels throughout the years. Hedge upkeep usually involves little more than watering, pruning, and trimming. Fences in cities and suburbs may attract graffiti, a most unwanted kind of attention; hedges, on the other hand, are seldom "tagged." A hedge lives and breathes, supports bird life, absorbs and filters pollutants, and cools the air; a fence does not provide these benefits.

Hedges serve not just as screens, but also as backdrops for other landscape features, like a curtain or the painted scenery behind an actor. Against a hedge, flowers are brighter, features such as fountains are highlighted, and the entire garden is framed.

Broadleaf evergreen screens

Broadleaf evergreen screens provide quick cover, growing up to 2 ft. per year. When kept in bounds, they hide the house next door, the school parking lot adjacent to your property, and your neighbor's outdoor grill. The most popular broadleaf evergreen shrubs—cherry laurel (*Prunus laurocerasus*), Portuguese laurel (*P. lusitanica*), Carolina laurel (*P. caroliniana*), and redtip (*Photinia ×fraseri*)—can be used to create tall, solid screens; they also grow into large trees about 30 ft. high and wide when left to their own devices. If you consider their growth habit, as with other hedge possibilities, and you find it appropriate for your space, a happy match results. If you choose a laurel for a fast cover-up, without considering your responsibility in maintaining it, you are asking for trouble.

A hedge with history

Grow a screen as old as the hills. Myrtle (*Myrtus communis*), bay laurel (*Laurus nobilis*), and boxwood (*Buxus sempervirens*) have been used as ornamental plants for thousands of years. The plants, their uses, and their power, are mentioned throughout literature and history. Roman generals who achieved a bloodless victory were crowned with myrtle. Apollo made bay laurel his sacred tree. The Romans were known to line coffins with sprays of box. Your hedge screen could become part of a very long story.

Myrtus communis, **common myrtle:** Dark green foliage, with white, fragrant flowers in summer followed by blackish fruit. 12 × 12 ft. 'Compacta' is smaller. Full sun. Zones 8–10.

Laurus nobilis, **bay laurel:** Fragrant, sturdy leaves. 15 × 15 ft. May grow larger in warm climates, to 35 × 20 ft. Full sun. Zones 8–11.

Buxus sempervirens, **boxwood:** Upright habit; flowers in spring. 20 × 20 ft. Full sun to part shade. Zones 5–9.

Conifer screens

Yew, Leyland cypress, and arborvitae are commonly chosen for hedges—and with good reason. The deep, dark foliage provides a finely textured backdrop for other plants and an evergreen screen that provides privacy.

A neatly clipped English yew (*Taxus baccata*) is the archetype of a formal hedge in all its glory. Hardy in Zones 6–8 (and Zone 5 with some protection), an English yew can be sheared into almost perfectly uniform shapes, such as a neat, boxy shapes; whimsical animal shapes; abstract forms; or even a teapot. Japanese yew (*Taxus cuspidata*) and the hybrid *T. ×media*, hardy to

Zone 4, offer myriad cultivars that exhibit characteristics such as shapes tall and thin or short and round, foliage of deep green or golden, and flowers and fruit. Japanese yew is tolerant of a variety of well-drained soils and can hold its own in an urban landscape.

Yew is not a fast-growing plant, so you need to plant many shrubs in the hedge, 18 to 24 in. apart, to achieve coverage during your lifetime. Although yew is a conifer, its fruit are not typical conifer cones; instead, it produces red berrylike fruits called *arils*, which appear on female plants. (Most, but not all, yews carry male and female flowers on separate plants.) The seed inside the aril, along with yew foliage and bark, are poisonous if ingested.

In 1888, a chance seedling cross between the Monterey cypress and Alaskan cedar was discovered at an estate in Wales. From almost that day, it seems, gardeners looking for a fast-growing hedge that can be sheared into shape have turned to the Leyland cypress (×*Cuprocyparis leylandii*, syn. ×*Cupressocyparis leylandii*) for the answer. Small cultivars now offer gardeners a more limited growth habit: 'Castlewellan', for example, grows to 40 × 10 ft. and features gold-tinted new growth.

The green mantle of a Leyland cypress hedge may provide the best screening option, but its fast growth means that two shearings per year may be required to maintain a formal shape.

OPPOSITE, TOP LEFT: Tall lilacs and a hedge screen two sides of a backyard hot tub area.
OPPOSITE, TOP RIGHT: A well pruned cherry laurel (*Prunus laurocerasus*) provides not just a screen, but also a backdrop for other plants in this front courtyard.
OPPOSITE, BOTTOM: Evergreen yew (*Taxus* spp.) hedges provide an informal backdrop for an ornamental garden and create an attractive screen.
ABOVE: Sheared yew hedges enclose a formal garden area.

Arborvitae

Arborvitae (*Thuja occidentalis*) deserves its own section, because it is one of the most useful—and often the most ill-used—hedge screen in the modern garden. Arborvitae may be the most-often planted privacy hedge. Popular selections of arborvitae, 'Smaragd' (also known as Emerald Green) and 'Holmstrup', do not grow into a solid hedge like yews or boxwoods; instead, each shrub is bullet shaped. Their advantages as hedge material lie in their size ('Smaragd' grows to 15 × 4 ft., and 'Holmstrup' is 10 × 2 ft.) and shape, and the fact that they rarely need pruning. Their advantages turn to disadvantages, however, when gardeners do not consider their narrow habit or other considerations while preparing and planting the shrubs.

High hedges and the law

We take our privacy seriously, but sometimes we may go overboard when trying to achieve it. After many complaints, legal problems, and even a neighborhood murder, the Antisocial Behavior Act of 2003 in Great Britain was written to include the problem of high hedges. Too many Leyland cypress hedges grew out of control, and the government deemed it necessary to provide a process by which a homeowner could file a complaint (as a last resort, after more congenial steps were attempted), because "his reasonable enjoyment of that property [was] being adversely affected by the height of a high hedge situated on land owned or occupied by another person."

Before you plant a tall hedge, consider who else will be affected by it. Sometimes good fences (or hedges) do not make good neighbors.

ABOVE, LEFT: A water feature in the garden provides an aural distraction and draws the eye away from unpleasant views. In the narrow space between two houses, a Leyland cypress (×*Cuprocyparis leylandii* 'Castlewellan') acts as a screen between the two properties.

ABOVE, RIGHT: Arborvitae, known for its rich green color, provides a short green hedge screen along a patio.

The longer the hedge, the more plants are required, and more arborvitae plants means more opportunities for something to go wrong. A 125 ft. row of arborvitae, for example, can turn from a sleek green wall into a gap-toothed file if one or more plants dies and must be removed. Arborvitae is considered a "quick-fix hedge," but it can lead to a big fix when the plants begin to fail as soon as they are removed from their containers. Too often, each plant is popped out of its pot and plopped into a hole. The roots circling around inside the nursery container continue to circle in a hole barely large enough to accommodate the mass. Eventually, without a spreading root system, the plant will be unable to take up sufficient water or withstand periods of drought. Circling roots can actually choke the plant to death if they wrap themselves around the plant's crown. Ripping roots apart can be a scary thing, but loosening the root ball at planting will help establish the plant. In a carelessly planted arborvitae hedge, the entire hedge can die off within a few years, so that crisp brown forms remain, often with the sales tags still attached. On uneven land, some plants may become waterlogged and drown in depressions and dry up on rises.

Overcrowding is not usually a problem with arborvitae; instead, the shrubs are often planted too far apart, so that even when they reach their mature size, gaps appear between each plant. You can avoid the spacing difficulty by planting arborvitae 2 to 3 ft. apart, instead of the often recommended 4 ft. Reduce the possibility of empty spots and relieve the visual monotony by breaking up the endless green with a section of fencing, a gate, or an opening or sheared archway onto a patio or with a sightline to a wall fountain or some artwork.

Although arborvitae looks compact, the upright branches of narrow-growing cultivars can be quite long. The branches emerge from the main stem and turn upward to develop that upright form. Often, after heavy snow or wind, or sometimes for no apparent reason, those ascending branches spread out like arms waving

Renovating a hedge

If a hedge grows too large to manage, and you find that your laurel screen has spread 10 ft. into your garden space, you may need to take drastic action and cut back 10 ft. all at once. Some plants tolerate radical renovation, and although they may look exposed for a while, the plants recover well. The best plants for radical renovation *break from old wood*—that is, the plant will put out new leaves from the trunk or other mature stems.

Carolina, cherry, and Portuguese laurels can be cut back hard, to large, ugly stubs; although recovery is not instantaneous, in a year or so they recover to appear smaller but healthy and leafy. To minimize the shock—to you, not to the plant—reduce the size of the shrub gradually, cutting back one side the first year, and then cutting back the other side and/or top the next year.

Hard-pruning should occur in early spring, so that the plants' roots have plenty of reserves on hand to incur new growth for the year. The best time to prune flowering shrubs is immediately after they flower. Although shrubs such as cherry and Portuguese laurel do flower, that is not normally their role in the landscape, so you do not need to be bound by that rule if you do not care about the flowers. No flowers means no fruit, which means no random reseeding.

Many hedge plants can be cut back hard to within a few inches of the ground. Such drastic pruning will sacrifice the function of the hedge for a few years, but the plants will grow back and can be maintained to restore their beauty. Before you start up the chain saw, however, imagine your landscape without that large green wall. Temporary though it is, a hard-pruned large hedge can look pretty shocking.

in the breeze. Your only option at that point is to cinch up the plant—wrap cord around it to tie the branches up into a vertical position. The cord may be noticeable, although over time some greenery will grow around it.

If your property of several acres needs hedging, the regular (and large) outline of *Thuja* 'Green Giant', a hybrid between western red cedar (*T. plicata*) and the Japanese *T. standishii*, will fit the bill and then some. 'Green Giant' grows 60 × 20 ft. in a broad pyramid shape. No pruning is needed, but you do need to be aware of overhead wires before you plant. Given the appropriate space, a line of 'Green Giant' arborvitaes marching down the road will be impressive, but a few of them squeezed between your patio and your neighbor's fence will be overkill.

Instead of planting arborvitae, consider planting a few conifers that grow shorter, horizontal side branches. Consider Italian cypress (*Cupressus sempervirens*), Serbian spruce (*Picea omorika*), oriental spruce (*P. orientalis* 'Skylands'), and umbrella pine (*Sciadopitys verticillata* 'Joe Kozey').

Maintaining a hedge

A formal hedge is an effective screening solution only when it is well maintained. An unmaintained cherry laurel is no longer an effective screen, but a large and spreading tree that encroaches on the garden. An untrimmed Leyland cypress quickly becomes the incredible hulk, swallowing everything in its path. A formal hedge should be sheared so that its sides are slightly sloped (unless the hedge is planted against a fence or wall and space is limited), with the bottom wider than the top; this keeps the top of the hedge from shading the lower foliage and ensures that the plants receive enough light to support new leafy growth, avoiding "bare legs."

Use an electric hedge trimmer to prune small-leaved plants, but, if possible, use hand shears for large-leaved plants to avoid ripping and shredding the leaves. A string stretched along the hedge will help guide your shears as you prune. If a hedge grows too large, prune one side hard one year and tackle the other side the next year. Take a little off the top each time.

Pleaching

In a pleached hedge, branches in a line of deciduous trees are woven together to form a solid hedge. A hedge of pleached trees is usually sheared so that front and back sides are smooth, forming a continual line of foliage and branches along the horizontal and vertical planes.

Pleached branches are not grafted together, but weave together as they grow. Branches are bent into place, and adjoining branches can be tied together to start growth in the desired direction. The tree canopies become the screen, with bare trunks below. A row of newly pleached trees can look similar to espaliered trees, although ornamental designs such as fans or cordons are not required.

When creating a pleached hedge, start with young trees with pliable branches, such as hornbeam (*Carpinus* spp.), beech (*Fagus* spp.), and linden (*Tilia* spp.) trees. Construct a frame by erecting posts or sturdy canes at the end of the row of trees and between trees. Run two or three horizontal rows of heavy-duty garden jute or wire at about 1 ft. intervals from post to post to use as a guide for the branches, which can be tied down loosely with tree ties. Branches of young trees often grow more heavily on one side or another; this will make it easier for you to orient the trees when planting, so that most branches grow in the same direction.

Each early spring, prune back any branches that do not grow along the row line. When the trees in the hedge reach the required height, bend the leader and tie it down as one of the branches. Remove the framework after two or three seasons, and you can continue to maintain the structure by securing branches with tree ties (which should be removed after a year of growth). Annual pruning is required for a pleached hedge.

Radical cuts work well for many hedge plants, including broadleaf evergreens such as English, Portuguese, and Carolina laurel (*Prunus laurocerasus*, *P. lusitanica*, and *P. caroliniana*) and deciduous plants including beech (*Fagus* spp.) and hornbeam (*Carpinus* spp.). Radical cuts are not recommended for most conifers; if you cut a branch into hard wood, a gap in the foliage will result. The coniferous exception is yew (*Taxus* spp.), which easily grows new leaves from old wood.

Selective pruning allows the shrub to retain some of its original form; this method takes patience, good tools, and a little know-how. Use selective pruning to maintain the natural form of a plant—even if it is a compact-growing selection, such as an arborvitae. The best hand tools for the job are bypass pruners, which are designed so that the cutting blade passes by a noncutting blade. These pruners cut the stem cleanly, as opposed to anvil-style pruners that smash the stem before cutting. Long-handled loppers, used for large branches, are available in both styles.

Before you begin pruning to shape a shrub, first remove the three Ds: dead, dying, and diseased branches. Then step back and look at the shrub; sometimes, this is all you need to do. If more pruning is needed, look for crossing branches or branches that extend into a pathway or otherwise look odd. Then look again at the entire shrub. You may need to remove far fewer branches than you first thought.

The stilt hedge

A stilt hedge can be created from trees or shrubs planted close together in a line. As suggested by its name, a stilt hedge is lifted clear of the ground, with lower branches trimmed 3 to 6 ft. up, and with 3 to 6 ft. of hedge above. Stilt hedges provide screening at a higher level, rather than all the way to the ground, leaving space for you to add more plants at ground level. Stilt hedges are usually maintained formally, with their canopies sheared in rectangular shapes or in small round

ABOVE, LEFT: A stilt hedge creates an attractive screen in a narrow space.
ABOVE, RIGHT: A tall pleached hedge lets in light under its canopy, where other plants can thrive.

canopies that resemble a row of lollipops. Stilt hedges are often pleached: the plants are trained to intertwine and provide a more solid hedge.

Less formally, a row of stilted shrubs or trees can be allowed to grow into their natural forms. You can create an informal stilt hedge using dwarf trees that mature at 8 to 20 ft., such as the compact river birch (*Betula nigra* 'Little King' or 'Studetec', sold as Tecumseh Compact) or selections of crape myrtle (*Lagerstroemia* spp.). In warmer regions (Zones 7-9), crape myrtles can be used for elegant limbed-up screens; their bark ages to a marbled mix of tan, pink, and gray. Many varieties offer a parade of color—summer panicles of flowers and warm autumn leaves. Look for the white-flowered *L.* 'Acoma', pink-flowered *L. indica* ×*fauriei* 'Hopi', and *L. indica* 'Watermelon Red', among many others that reach about 12 ft.

In a sunny area beneath a stilt hedge, plant spring bulbs and low-growing perennials. Take advantage of the space by including a swath of daffodils, a blanket of hardy cyclamen, or soft mounds of hardy geranium, such as *Geranium* ×*oxonianum* 'Wargrave Pink', which can reseed itself to create a ground cover.

The bamboo screen

Few plant topics provoke such extreme opinions as the topic of using bamboo in the garden: gardeners either love it or hate it. Those who hate it often complain about neighbors who let their bamboo spread with abandon or previous homeowners who planted it with no regard for how far it would spread. Lovers of bamboo, meanwhile, expound on its usefulness as a screen, the sound of the breeze hissing through its leaves, and the virtues of having a source of bamboo stakes to use in the garden.

In addition to its usefulness as food (for humans and pandas) and as a building material, bamboo can be used to create a lush, living screen in the garden. Its stems, or culms, can be colorful, and the joints, or nodes, on the culms and branches add character. Its dense growth provides a textural feast. Although evergreen, bamboo drops its leaves as it grows, and a thick stand creates a humus-filled layer on the soil.

Containing uncontained bamboo

Containing bamboo that was planted without a barrier, or when a barrier has failed, is a big job. The surest way to remove bamboo is the hardest way: Dig up all the rhizomes that spread out from the area (follow the rhizome "trail" from the point you cut), and carefully monitor a wide area throughout the year and for years to come, breaking or cutting off any new growth to starve the root system. Bamboo emerging in a lawn can be mowed. Bamboo rhizomes may grow 20 ft. in a single year, so clearing out escaped bamboo is no small feat.

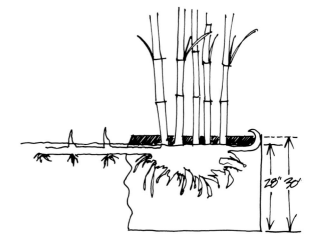

ABOVE: You must bury thick plastic 28 to 30 in. under the soil to create a deep barrier around the rhizomes and prevent running bamboo from spreading far and wide.

The world of bamboo is large, but your requirements for bamboo as a screen narrows the field of choices considerably. In a city or suburban garden, for example, a stand of timber bamboo, such as *Phyllostachys bambusoides*, would not be suitable. This is not the bamboo to plant as a screen around your deck. Timber bamboo can grow up to 50 ft., with a culm diameter of 6 in., and because it is a running bamboo, if its root system (rhizomes) is uncontained, it will spread far and wide and is nearly impossible to control.

ABOVE: Tall bamboo will fill in to provide a light screen above the fence level in this urban garden.

Better to look to a more reasonable selection for a city lot, such as clumping bamboo, whose rhizomes spread slowly and do not run underground to sprout in the middle of your neighbor's driveway. Blue fountain bamboo (*Fargesia nitida*), for example, reaches about 15 ft., with a culm diameter of 3/4 in. and a soft visual texture and, true to its name, fountainlike form.

Timber bamboo and other species in the genus *Phyllostachys*, such as black bamboo (*P. nigra*), are considered running bamboo, and the plants in the genus *Fargesia* are clumping bamboo. The difference between the two is important. Running bamboo sends out long, underground rhizomes that can grow 30 ft. or more away from the original plant. Along the rhizome at varying intervals, upright culms grow. The culms of

clumping bamboo grow from rhizomes, too, but they are shorter and grow more slowly, so the stems arise from a congested center rather than spreading out. Clumping bamboo usually has a vase-shaped form.

Unless you are willing to prepare your garden to accommodate long-term confinement of the plant, choose clumping bamboo. In addition to *Fargesia nitida*, other clumpers include *F. robusta*, *F. dracocephala* 'Rufa', and umbrella bamboo (*F. murielae*). All will grow from 10 to 15 ft., with lovely culms, and they stay close to where you plant them.

If you plant running bamboo in the ground, you should, at the least, install a strong and long-lasting bamboo barrier, which is made of sturdy, high-density polyethylene plastic sheets (HDPE), 60 to 80 mil. (0.06 to 0.08 in.) thick. Each plastic wall should be installed 28 to 30 in. below the soil. The barrier must also extend 2 to 4 in. above the soil line and be bent outward; this makes it easy for you to see any rhizomes that attempt an escape—otherwise, the rhizomes will hop over and be on their merry way. A few inches of black plastic may not be the most attractive feature in your garden, but it is probably necessary if you plant running bamboo. In

ABOVE: Clumping bamboo can be grown as screens in sturdy containers in city gardens with little or no ground to plant.
OPPOSITE: A collection of containers planted with conifers, bamboo, and perennials provides not only a screen between the rooftop garden and other buildings, but also a more private garden space.
PAGE 121: With lush container dividers between two angled seating areas, the spaces can feel entirely separate.

scary movies, the hero bolts the door against the monster, and then wipes his or her brow with relief, unaware that the monster is creeping through an unlocked window. Bamboo is like that monster, only in a leafy green way. Never assume that a barrier for a running bamboo will keep it contained forever.

Another method of containing running bamboo relies on your vigilance. After you plant a row of bamboo, dig a trench on either side of the row of plants, 12 in. deep and at least 4 in. wide, and filled with wood chips or rocks. This will act as a sort of moat. Every spring and fall, police the borders and cut out rhizomes that begin to grow into the no-grow zone.

You might think that a pot or planter will keep bamboo contained, but think again. Clumping bamboo is suitable for pots or planters, but it will eventually crowd the container and need to be removed and divided. Running bamboo is another story, although some gardeners swear that even running bamboo can be contained in planters. With continual rhizome pruning, you may be able to keep running bamboo inside a container, but it involves removing the plant from the container and removing some rhizomes, of course. Even with that effort, running bamboo can still break out—or even break through a container—when you are not looking.

Screens in containers

If your apartment balcony is only 15 ft. from the balcony in the next building, or the boundaries of your rooftop patio need to be screened with a comforting line of small trees, shrubs, and perennials, you can use screens, too. Plants on balconies, patios, and rooftops can screen unfortunate views and buffer the vibrant city environment of neon, noise, and traffic.

Create groupings of containerized plants at particularly vulnerable points. A corner grouping of plants in containers provides a screen that hides a view from the neighboring building into your space. An arrangement created behind a seating area with a view of the city beyond can block the view into your private space. A light bamboo or rush screen, in addition to a planted screen, will take advantage of the site to help create a garden and a space for entertaining guests, while letting you enjoy the city environment without feeling swallowed up by it.

How bamboo grows

After you plant bamboo, it takes time to establish. Young plantings sport thin culms; the diameter of the emerging culms is their diameter at maturity. As the bamboo plant matures, emerging culms will eventually appear in the expected thickness. Like any other plant, bamboo does not instantly grow to its ultimate height. Bamboo needs to establish its root system before it puts energy into top growth.

You might have heard that when one bamboo (of a particular species) blooms, every plant of that species around the world will bloom at the same time, and then they will all die, because they have all been propagated from the same plant. The truth is more complicated, however. It appears likely that when one bamboo plant flowers, many others will flower as well. A bamboo that flowers may die, but it can also survive.

If you grow plants in containers, remember that they require more attention than in-ground plants, which get much of the water and nutrients they need by sending out roots far and wide. In a container, plant roots can grow only so far. Containerized plants receive water from rain or you (by hand or via an automated system) and nutrients from the potting medium or the appropriate levels of fertilizers that you apply. As a rule of thumb, if a plant is to remain in a container for some time, you should cut doses of fertilizer in half—no need to encourage rampant growth.

Plants can and will outgrow their containers. For that reason, you should repot containerized plants every few years. You know that it is time to repot a plant when water runs quickly through the soil, the soil never seems to stay moist, and the soil pulls away from the sides of the pot—all of which indicate that the plant's roots are overtaking the planting medium. If each year's foliage on container-grown trees and shrubs seems smaller, the plants need to be repotted. For a fresh start, pull out the plants, prune the roots, add new potting soil to the container, and repot.

PLANT LISTS

Reading about, shopping for, and finding the right plants for the garden is a joy. But plants are not inanimate objects, so you should bear in mind the characteristics of their function and beauty as you begin the hunt. You can easily measure a sofa to determine whether it will fit into your living room, but trying to measure a living, breathing plant to determine whether it will fit in your garden is an entirely different exercise. The books might say it will grow to 15 ft., and 99 of 100 of those same plants may grow to 15 ft., but it is not out of the realm of possibility that yours will grow to 18 ft., or 12 ft. Take all height and width *guidelines* for what they are.

Check your state and local noxious weed list. An invasive plant in California may not be so named in Connecticut. Invasiveness is a regional issue, but some plants can be considered a nuisance even after years of staying put as an ornamental in a region. Read more at www.invasives.org.

Zones, too, seem to be negotiable at times. The zones listed here are from the USDA hardiness zone map, based on the average minimum temperature. Remember that within your city, town, and garden are microclimates that might allow something just out of your area's zone to grow—or that might damage a plant considered within your area's planting zone. Minimum temperature is only one, albeit one important, way of thinking about what you can grow in your garden. Consider other aspects of the garden as well, including the soil type and texture, rainfall patterns, and topography. Throughout the following pages, plant lists offer ideas to consider for your garden.

- Evergreen shrubs
- Plants for hedgerows
- Plants for seaside gardens
- Plants for windy sites
- Thorny plants
- Crab apples
- Broadleaf evergreens
- No-shear hedge plants
- Narrow plants
- Small trees
- Vines for trellises

EVERGREEN SHRUBS

A variety of evergreen shrubs can be planted to fit a variety of situations, whether to provide a buffer in a terraced garden or to hold a year-round presence in hedges, mixed plantings around hedges, and containers.

Camellia sasanqua
Sasanqua camellia
Glossy, dark green foliage; winter flowers can be damaged by unusual freezes. 'Apple Blossom', semi-double white with pink edges. 'Setsugekka', single white flowers. 'Yuletide', single red flowers. 10 × 10 ft. Sun to part shade. Zones 7–9.

Chamaecyparis obtusa
hinoki cypress
Small mounding growers with green ('Nana'), golden ('Nana Aurea'), or dark green ('Nana Gracilis') foliage. 3 × 3 ft. Full sun to part shade. Zones 4–8.

Cistus ×hybridus (syn. Cistus ×corbariensis)
rock rose
Dark gray-green foliage; pink buds with white flowers in late spring. 3 × 5 ft. Full sun, sharp drainage. Zones 7–10.

Cistus ×skanbergii
rock rose
Gray-green foliage; pink flowers in late spring. 3 × 5 ft. Full sun, sharp drainage. Zones 7–10.

Ilex crenata
Japanese holly
'Helleri', evergreen with small, dark green foliage, 4 × 5 ft.
'Northern Beauty', evergreen with small, glossy, dark green foliage, 4 × 4 ft. Full sun to part shade. Zones 6–9.

Lonicera pileata
boxleaf honeysuckle
Horizontal branches, with small, glossy leaves; unnoticeable flowers followed by dark purple, berry-like fruit. 2 × 8 ft. Full sun to part shade. Zones 5–9.

Pittosporum tenuifolium
'Golf Ball'
Green foliage with a sheen; black stems. 3 × 3 ft. Full sun to part shade. Zones 8–11.

Thuja plicata 'Whipcord'
dwarf western red cedar
Unusual foliage of long, thin, cascading tendrils. 5 × 4 ft. Full sun to part shade. Zones 5–8.

Thujopsis dolabrata 'Nana'
dwarf hiba cedar
Conifer with thick sprays of green foliage with white undersides. 4 × 6 ft. Full sun to part shade. Zones 5–9.

Vaccinium ovatum
evergreen huckleberry
Evergreen, with pink spring flowers and summer fruit. 5 × 5 ft. Part shade to shade. Zones 7–9.

Vaccinium 'Sunshine Blue'
dwarf blueberry
Evergreen, with midsummer fruit. 4 × 4 ft. Full sun to part shade. Zones 5–10.

PLANTS FOR HEDGEROWS

When you are considering hedgerow plants for the small garden, include plants that do not quickly outgrow their space, unless regular maintenance is an accepted part of your gardening chores. Hedgerow plants can be regularly cropped, stooled, or renovated, but clipping and reclipping several times a year to clear a path along the side of the house can be a frustrating chore.

Avoid weedy reseeders, such as plants on noxious weed lists or just plain obnoxious plants—some are a headache to maintain if they spread easily. Yes, offer fruited shrubs to the birds, but do so with caution. Remember that bird droppings include seeds from fruiting shrubs, which means that the birds may spread unwanted plants around your garden in unexpected places. Avoid plants that are invasive in your area; to find out more, you can visit websites such as www.invasive.org.

Choose from among native plants, near natives, and plants that grow well in your region. If you have room, include a small tree here and there to vary the height. Include one or two of your favorite small conifers or berried shrubs.

Regions with cold winters and hot summers: Zones 3–6

Amelanchier arborea and **A. canadensis**
serviceberry
Deciduous, with small clusters of white, star-shaped flowers in spring and blue berries in early summer; red-orange fall color. 25 × 25 ft. Full sun to part shade. Zones 4–9.

Ceanothus americanus
New Jersey tea
Deciduous, with clusters of tiny white flowers in spring. 4 × 5 ft. Full sun to part shade. Zones 4–8.

Clethra alnifolia
summersweet
Deciduous, with 6 in. spikes of tiny, white, fragrant flowers in summer; tolerates wet soil. 'Hummingbird', 4 × 4 ft. 'Ruby Spice', pink flowers, 8 × 6 ft. Part shade to shade. Zones 3–9.

Ostrya virginiana
hop hornbeam
Deciduous, seeds carried in papery pods that resemble hops. 40 × 30 ft. Full sun to part shade. Zones 3–9.

Viburnum dentatum
arrowwood
Deciduous, with 4 in. wide, flat-topped clusters of white flowers in late spring followed by dark blue fruit. 10 × 10 ft. 'Christom' (Blue Muffin), 5 × 5 ft. Full sun to part shade. Zones 2–8. Also try nannyberry (*Viburnum lentago*).

Viburnum prunifolium
black haw
Deciduous, with 4 in. wide, flat-topped clusters of white flowers in late spring followed by dark blue fruit that attracts birds in winter. 15 × 12 ft. Full sun to part shade. Zones 3–9.

U.S. Pacific Northwest and Northern California coast: Zones 7–9

Amelanchier alnifolia
western serviceberry or saskatoon
Deciduous, with small, strappy white flowers in spring followed by blue fruit. 20 × 20 ft. 'Obelisk', 15 × 4 ft. Full sun to part shade. Zones 2–8.

Ceanothus impressus
California lilac
Evergreen, with small, dark green crinkled leaves and clusters of tiny blue flowers in mid to late spring. 5 × 8 ft. 'Julia Phelps', 6 × 6 ft. 'Puget Blue', 10 × 10 ft. Full sun. Zones 8–11. Many other selections available.

Garrya elliptica
silk tassel bush
Evergreen leaves with wavy margins; male plants have 6–8 in. late-winter catkins. 12 × 12 ft. 'James Roof', with catkins to 12 in. Full sun. Zones 8–11. Also G. *fremontii* (fever bush) and G. ×*issaquahensis*

Mahonia aquifolium
Oregon grape
Evergreen, glossy leaves tipped with soft spines are tinted red in winter; clusters of fragrant yellow flowers in spring followed by blue fruit. 6 × 5 ft. 'Compactum', to 3 ft. Full sun to part shade. Zones 5–8.

Morella californica (syn. *Myrica californica*)
California wax myrtle
Evergreen, with narrow, aromatic leaves; vertical stems rise like pillars. Insignificant flowers followed by fruit attached directly to stem. Good wildlife habitat. Can be pruned to shape. 15 × 10 ft. Full sun. Zones 7–9.

Ribes sanguineum
flowering currant
Deciduous, with variable fall color. Clusters of pink flowers begin to appear in late winter and last well into spring; attracts hummingbirds. Blue fruit. 'King Edward VII', pink-red flowers. 6 × 6 ft. Full sun to part shade. Zones 6–9.

Rosa nutkana
Nootka rose
Deciduous, suckering rose, with single pink flowers 3 in. across and red-brown hips. 'Plena' (syn. *R. californica* 'Plena') has double flowers. 8 × 8 ft. Full sun. Zones 3–9.

Sambucus racemosa
red elderberry
Deciduous, with cone-shaped, white flowers in spring followed by red fruit. 10 × 10 ft. Full sun to part shade. Zones 3–8.

Desert regions: Zones 8–10

Acacia constricta
whitethorn acacia
Deciduous tree; thorny, with yellow-orange flowers in spring. 15 × 15 ft. Full sun. Zones 6–10.

Chilopsis linearis
desert willow
Deciduous tree, with pink, funnel-shaped, scented flowers throughout summer. 25 × 25 ft. Full sun. Zones 7–10.

Echinocactus spp.
barrel cactus
Slow-growing cactus with yellow or magenta flowers, depending on species. 4 × 2 ft. Full sun. Zones 9–11.

Epilobium canum subsp. *latifolium*
hummingbird trumpet
Spreading perennial with red-orange flowers in late summer. 2 ft. Full sun. Zones 7–10.

Fouquieria splendens
ocotillo
Cactus with thin, upright stems; leaves drop during periods of no water and sprout when moisture is available; scarlet flowers may appear at tips after rainfall. 15 × 15 ft. Full sun. Zones 9–11.

Mimosa dysocarpa
velvetpod mimosa
Deciduous shrub with pink and white flowers in summer. 6 × 6 ft. Full sun. Zones 8–11.

Stenocereus thurberi
organ pipe cactus
Cactus with white to pink flowers. 4–20 ft. Full sun. Zones 9–12.

Tecoma stans
yellow trumpet bush
Evergreen shrub with yellow flowers through summer. 15 × 10 ft. Full sun. Zones 9–11.

U.S. Southeast, Gulf Coast, and mid and lower South: Zones 8–10

Carpinus caroliniana
American hornbeam
Deciduous tree; male and female catkins followed by winged fruit. 35 × 35 ft. Full sun to part shade. Zones 3–9.

Clethra alnifolia
summersweet
Deciduous, with 6 in. spikes of tiny, fragrant flowers in summer; tolerates wet soil. To 16 ft. 'Hummingbird', dwarf form, with white flowers, 4 × 4 ft. 'Ruby Spice', with pink flowers, 8 × 6 ft. Part shade to shade. Zones 3–9.

Crataegus opaca
mayhaw
Deciduous; early spring flowers followed by fruit in midspring. 40 × 40 ft. Full sun to part shade. Zones 8–11.

Diospyros virginiana
persimmon
Deciduous; fragrant spring flowers followed by orange fruit that persists on tree. Male and female flowers may appear on separate plants. 35 × 35 ft. Full sun. Zone 4–9.

Ilex opaca
American holly
Evergreen, with white spring flowers followed by persistent red berries. Male and female flowers appear on separate plants. Many selections include 'Jersey Knight' (male) and 'Jersey Princess' (female). 30 × 20 ft. Full sun to part shade. Zones 5–9.

Ostrya virginiana
hop hornbeam
Deciduous; seeds carried in papery pods that resemble hops. 40 × 30 ft. Full sun to part shade. Zones 3–9.

Sassafras albidum
sassafras
Deciduous; male and female flowers appear on separate plants. Green flowers in spring followed by black fruit on female plants. 60 × 40 ft. Full sun to part shade. Zones 4–9.

U.S. Mid-Atlantic Coast: Zones 5–7

Aralia spinosa
devil's walking stick
Deciduous; large compound leaves with spines on branches and leaf stems. Large clusters of flowers in spring followed by black fruit. 20 × 10 ft. Full sun to part shade. Zones 4–9.

Callicarpa americana
beautyberry
Deciduous; clusters of pink flowers in spring followed by persistent lavender berries close to stem. 6 × 6 ft. Full sun to part shade. Zones 6–10.

Ceanothus americanus
New Jersey tea
Deciduous, with clusters of tiny white flowers in spring. 4 × 5 ft. Full sun to part shade. Zones 4–8.

Cornus alternifolia
pagoda dogwood
Deciduous shrub; compound leaves held on horizontal branches. White flower clusters develop into black berries. 30 × 30 ft. Full sun to part shade. Zones 3–8.

Magnolia virginiana
sweetbay magnolia
Evergreen to semi-evergreen, with white, fragrant flowers in late spring and sporadically through summer. 20 × 20 ft. Full sun to part shade. Zones 5–10.

Physocarpus opulifolius
ninebark
Deciduous; clusters of white to pink flowers in spring followed by red fruit. 8 × 6 ft. Full sun to part shade. Zones 2–8.

Quercus ilicifolia
bear oak
Deciduous; acorns less than 1/2 in. long. 15 × 15 ft. Full sun to part shade. Zones 3–7.

Viburnum dentatum
arrowwood
Deciduous, with 4 in. wide, flat-topped clusters of white flowers in late spring followed by dark blue fruit. 10 × 10 ft. 'Christom' (Blue Muffin), 5 × 5 ft. Full sun to part shade. Zones 2–8. Also try nannyberry (*V. lentago*).

U.S. Northeast: Zones 3–5

Amelanchier arborea and *A. canadensis*
serviceberry
Deciduous, with small clusters of star-shaped white flowers in spring followed by blue berries in June; red-orange fall foliage. 25 × 25 ft. Full sun to part shade. Zones 4–9.

Ceanothus americanus
New Jersey tea
Deciduous, with clusters of tiny white flowers in spring. 4 × 5 ft. Full sun to part shade. Zones 4–8.

Ostrya virginiana
hop hornbeam
Deciduous; seeds carried in papery pods that resemble hops. 40 × 30 ft. Full sun to part shade. Zones 3–9.

Viburnum dentatum
arrowwood
Deciduous, with 4 in. wide, flat-topped clusters of white flowers in late spring followed by dark blue fruit. 10 × 10 ft. 'Christom' (Blue Muffin), 5 × 5 ft. Full sun to part shade. Zones 2–8. Also try nannyberry (*V. lentago*).

Viburnum prunifolium
black haw
Deciduous, with 4 in. wide, flat-topped clusters of white flowers in late spring followed by dark blue fruit that attracts birds in winter. 15 × 12 ft. Full sun to part shade. Zones 3–9.

PLANTS FOR SEASIDE GARDENS

Many plants that tolerate salt spray on their foliage also tolerate a fair amount of wind—and "tolerate" in this case means they still look reasonably good. Not all wind-tolerant plants are salt-tolerant plants. Many great plants can be used in a seaside garden. You will find more plants—and some contradictions—from the vast sources online. Look for plants native to your local beaches for a natural habitat.

Seaside trees

Acer campestre
hedge maple
Dark green, shallowly lobed leaves. Good shearing hedge plant. 25 × 25 ft. Full sun to part shade. Zones 5–8.

Ginkgo biloba
ginkgo, maidenhair tree
Deciduous, with fan-shaped, green leaves that turn bright yellow in the fall. Male trees produce catkins in spring and females produce messy, odorous seed pods. Better to plant male trees. 80 × 40 ft. Zones 3–8.

Magnolia virginiana
sweetbay magnolia
Evergreen to semi-evergreen, with white, fragrant flowers in late spring and sporadically through summer. 20 × 20 ft. Full sun to part shade. Zones 5–10.

Olea europaea
common olive
Evergreen, with gray-green foliage and smooth bark. Fruit drops in late summer. 30 × 25 ft. Fruitless selections are available: 'Montra' (Little Ollie), dwarf, to 6 × 6 ft. 'Monher' (Majestic Beauty), 30 × 25 ft. Full sun. Zones 8–11.

Pinus contorta var. *contorta*
shore pine
Conifer with wide-spreading branches, often curving trunk. 35 × 35 ft. Full sun. Zones 3–9.

Pinus heldreichii (syn. *P. leucodermis*)
Bosnian pine
Conifer with pyramidal form; upright branches mature to a layered appearance. 25 × 12 ft. 'Irish Bell', 8 × 5 ft. Full sun. Zones 3–8.

Pinus mugo
dwarf mountain pine
Conifer; often multi-stemmed. Not for hot, humid regions. 20 × 30 ft. 'Mops', 4 × 4 ft. Full sun. Zones 2–8.

Pinus thunbergii
Japanese black pine
Conifer with dark green needles and dark purple fissured bark. 60 × 20 ft. 'Pygmaea', 5 × 5 ft. Full sun. Zones 5–8.

Quercus ilex
holm oak
Evergreen, with smooth bark. Dense canopy can be thinned. Often smaller in cultivation. 60 × 60 ft. Full sun. Zones 7–9.

Ulmus parvifolia
Chinese elm
Deciduous or semi-evergreen, with flaky bark in orange, tan, and gray. 50 × 40 ft. 'Seiju', 10 × 10 ft. Full sun. Zones 5–9.

Umbellularia californica
California bay laurel
Evergreen with narrow, aromatic leaves, and small clusters of white flowers. Can be used as sheared hedge, but odor from bruised or cut foliage can cause headaches. 25 × 25 ft. Zones 7–9.

Seaside shrubs

Arbutus unedo
strawberry tree
Evergreen, with dark green serrated leaves, and white heatherlike flowers in autumn as bumpy red fruit ripens; cinnamon-colored bark. 25 × 25 ft. 'Compacta', to 15 × 15 ft. 'Elfin King', to 5 ft. Full sun to part shade. Zones 7–9.

Aronia melanocarpa
black chokeberry
Deciduous, with smooth-edged, spoon-shaped leaves, and white flowers in spring followed by clusters of dark berries in fall. Tolerates continually wet soil, and can sucker to form a thicket. 6 × 6 ft. 'Autumn Magic', 6 × 7 ft., has good fall color. 'Morton' (Iriquois), 3 × 5 ft. Full sun. Zones 3–8.

Caragana arborescens
Siberian pea tree
Deciduous, often multi-stemmed with compound leaves and clusters of yellow pealike flowers in spring; peapods develop in summer. 20 × 15 ft. Zones 2–8.

Cistus ×hybridus
white rock rose
Evergreen, with white flowers from pink buds in mid to late spring. 3 × 5 ft. Others include brown-eyed rock rose (*C. ladanifer*), 5 × 5 ft., and pink *C. ×skanbergii*, 3 × 3 ft. Full sun. Zones 7–10.

Escallonia rubra
red escallonia
Evergreen, with small, rough leaves and clusters of small, tubular, red-pink flowers throughout the year, mostly in summer; can be sheared. 15 × 15 ft. Many hybrids and cultivars include rose-colored 'Pride of Donard', 5 × 8 ft., and 'Apple Blossom', 8 × 8 ft. Full sun. Zones 8–10.

Griselinia littoralis
New Zealand broadleaf
Evergreen with glossy, round leaves; tolerates shearing. 'Variegata' leaves are irregularly marked with creamy white. 25 × 15 ft. Full sun. Zones 7–9.

Hippophae rhamnoides
sea buckthorn
Deciduous, with silver leaves; orange berries appear to be attached directly to stem. Both male and female plants needed for fruit set. 25 × 25 ft. 'Sprite', 2 ft. Full sun. Zones 4–8.

Ilex vomitoria
yaupon holly
Evergreen with small leaves. 20 × 12 ft. 'Schillings' (Stokes Dwarf), 4 × 4 ft. 'Will Fleming', 15 × 2 ft. Full sun. Zones 5–8.

Lantana camara
lantana
Deciduous; leaves feel rough. Clusters of small, often two-toned flowers throughout summer are attractive to butterflies. 6 × 6 ft. Many other selections include 'American Red', to 6 ft. 'Miss Huff' is slightly more hardy, to 6 ft. Full sun. Zones 7–11.

Lavandula spp.
lavender
Perennial with aromatic gray leaves and spikes of lavender flowers in summer. Also French lavender (*L. dentata*), Spanish lavender (*L. stoechas*), and English lavender (*L. ×intermedia*). 3 × 3 ft. Full sun. Zones 6–9.

Leptospermum scoparium
New Zealand tea tree
Evergreen with needlelike foliage; small open flowers in shades of pink appear in late spring. 8 × 8 ft. 'Appleblossom' is a light pink double. 'Crimson Glory' is dark pink. (Nanum Group) 'Ruru', is a dwarf, to 2 ft., with flowers with dark eyes. Full sun. Zones 9–11.

Morella californica (syn. *Myrica californica*)
California wax myrtle
Evergreen, with narrow, aromatic leaves; vertical stems rise like pillars. Insignificant flowers followed by fruit attached directly to stem. Good wildlife habitat. Can be pruned to shape. 15 × 10 ft. Full sun. Zones 7–9.

Myrtus communis
common myrtle
Evergreen with dark green foliage; white fragrant flowers in summer, followed by blackish fruit. 12 × 12 ft. 'Compacta' is smaller, to 3 × 3 ft. Full sun. Zones 8–10. Related species *Luma apiculata* has flaky, cinnamon-colored bark, and may grow to 40 ft. but is usually more shrubby. Zones 8–11.

Pittosporum tobira
Japanese mock orange
Evergreen with spoon-shaped leaves; clusters of fragrant white flowers in early spring. Grows best and largest in mild, warm climates. 'Variegata' has white-edged leaves. 15 × 18 ft. Full sun. Zones 8–10.

Potentilla fruticosa
cinquefoil
Deciduous, with small leaves. Flowers over a long period. Not for hot, humid climates. 'Abbottswood' has white flowers. 'Coronation Triumph' has bright yellow flowers. 4 × 4 ft. Full sun. Zones 2–8.

Rhaphiolepis 'Montic' (Majestic Beauty)
Indian hawthorn
Evergreen with pink flowers. 25 × 10 ft. Full sun. Zones 8–11.

Rhaphiolepis umbellata 'Rutraph1' (Southern Moon)
dwarf Indian hawthorn
Evergreen with thick, glossy leaves and small white flowers in spring. 5 × 6 ft. Full sun. Zones 8–11.

Rosa rugosa 'Scabrosa'
scabrosa rose
Deciduous with bristly, spiny stems. Repeat flowering with fragrant, single, large magenta flowers followed by "tomato" hips. Tolerates poor soil. 5 × 6 ft. Full sun. Zones 2–9.

Rosmarinus officinalis
rosemary
Evergreen with aromatic, needlelike foliage and blue flowers held close to stem in winter. 6 × 4 ft. Full sun. Zones 8–10. 'Arp', hardy to Zone 7.

Sabal minor
dwarf palmetto
Fan-shaped palm with leaves to 5 ft. across. 6 × 6 ft. Full sun. Zones 8–10.

Trachycarpus fortunei
windmill palm
Fan-shaped palm with leaves to 3 ft. across. 10 × 6 ft. Full sun. Zones 7–10.

Viburnum tinus 'Spring Bouquet'
laurustinus
Evergreen with leathery leaves; domes of pink-tinged, fragrant flowers in late winter, followed by blue fruit. 6 × 8 ft. Full sun to part shade. Zones 7–9.

Seaside perennials and grasses

Armeria maritima
sea thrift
Tight clumps of grassy foliage; stalks with round clusters of pink flowers in summer. 'Bloodstone' has dark pink flowers. 1 × 1 ft. Full sun. Zones 4–8.

Aster novae-angliae
New England aster
Tall stalks with autumn flowers. 'Andenken an Alma Pötschke' has deep pink flowers. 4 × 4 ft. Full sun. Zones 4–8.

Aster novi-belgii
Michaelmas daisy
Late summer flowers in range of colors. 'Coombe Fishacre' has lilac flowers. 'Professor Anton Kippenberg' has magenta flowers. 2 × 2 ft. Full sun. Zones 4–8.

Bergenia spp.
pigsqueak
Large, glossy succulent leaves usually evergreen; short stalks of pink flowers in early spring. Foliage turns maroon in winter on *B.* 'Bressingham Ruby'. Also *B. cordifolia* 'Winterglut'. 18 × 18 in. Full sun to part shade. Zones 4–8.

Calamagrostis ×*acutiflora* 'Overdam'
silver reed grass
Herbaceous grass with narrow leaves with thin white stripe; suffers in heat and humidity. Should be cut down at end of winter. 'Karl Foerster' similar but without variegation. 5 × 2 ft. Full sun. Zones 4–9.

Elymus magellanicus
blue Magellan grass
Herbaceous grass, with steel-blue foliage; suffers in heat and humidity. Cut down at end of winter. 2 × 2 ft. Full sun. Zones 4–8.

Gaillardia spp.
blanket flower
Summer daisylike flowers in shades of yellow, orange, and bronze; selections include yellow-red 'Fanfare' and red 'Commotion'. 3 × 2 ft. Full sun. Zones 3–10.

Helictotrichon sempervirens
blue oat grass
Steel-blue evergreen foliage. 3 × 3 ft. Full sun. Zones 4–8.

Miscanthus sinensis
maidenhair grass
Herbaceous grass with late-season flowers. 'Morning Light' has white leaf margins, 5 × 4 ft. 'Yaku-jima' slightly smaller, 4 × 3 ft. Full sun. Zones 5–10.

Pennisetum alopecuroides 'Hameln'
pink fountain grass
Herbaceous grass with pinkish flower heads in summer. 'Moudry', black fountain grass, has dark mauve flower heads. 3 × 3 ft. Full sun to part shade. Zones 5–9.

Perovskia atriplicifolia
Russian sage
Silver-blue airy aromatic foliage, with spikes of lavender flowers in summer. 4 × 4 ft. Full sun. Zones 5–9.

Rudbeckia fulgida var. *sullivantii* 'Goldsturm'
black-eyed Susan
Midsummer yellow-orange flowers with dark centers above dark leaves. 3 × 2 ft. Full sun. Zones 3–9.

Stachys byzantina
lambs' ears
Soft, aromatic, silver-gray lower leaves form a mat below small, magenta flowers on tall stalks. 2 × 2 ft.

'Big Ears' is slightly smaller with no flowers, leaves more gray-green. Full sun. Zones 4-9.

Veronica spicata 'Rotfuchs'
red fox speedwell
Spikes of red-pink flowers in summer. Many varieties conducive to seaside gardens. 18 × 18 in. Full sun. Zones 3-8.

PLANTS FOR WINDY SITES

What helps a plant tolerate wind? Plants with flexible stems and branches are more likely to bend than break in the wind, and those able to flush out new growth when tops or branches do break off can sustain and recover from damage. If a plant's foliage is not too dense, wind can pass through the plant instead of bouncing off it. Windbreak plants filter and soften the wind, making them the perfect buffers. Although many deciduous plants tolerate wind, some need protection from wind in winter; this list includes only evergreens, both conifers and broadleaf plants. When planting a windbreak, a shrub row on the windward side of a row of trees can help divert the wind up and over the garden and house.

Conifers for windy sites

Calocedrus decurrens
incense cedar
Rich green fans of foliage, with red bark. 50 × 10 ft. 'Compacta', to 6 ft. 'Aureovariegata' has bright yellow foliage. Full sun. Zones 5-8.

Cupressus arizonica
Arizona cypress
Green to silvery foliage. Not for humid regions. 50 × 30 ft. *Cupressus arizonica* var. *glabra* 'Carolina Sapphire', 30 × 20 ft.; *C. arizonica* var. *glabra* 'Silver Smoke', 15 × 8 ft. Full sun. Zones 6-11.

Cupressus sempervirens
Italian cypress
Short, mostly horizontal or slightly ascending branches. 60 × 6 ft. Look for Stricta Group for narrowest form. 'Tiny Tower', 25 × 3 ft. 'Swane's Gold', with golden yellow new growth, 20 × 3 ft. Full sun. Zones 7-10.

Juniperus scopulorum 'Moonglow'
Rocky Mountain juniper
Dense blue-gray foliage. Not for humid regions. 20 × 5 ft. Full sun. Zones 4-8.

Juniperus virginiana
eastern red cedar
Blue-green foliage. Alternate host for apple cedar rust; do not plant near orchards. 'Canaertti', 25 × 15 ft. 'Emerald Sentinel', 20 × 8 ft. Full sun. Zones 4-9.

Picea omorika
Serbian spruce
Dark green needles with blue undersides; slow-growing. 50 × 20 ft. 'Nana' is a more rounded dwarf form, to 10 ft. Full sun. Zones 4-8.

Pinus contorta var. *contorta*
shore pine
Wide-spreading branches, often curving trunk. 35 × 35 ft. Full sun. Zones 3-9.

Broadleaf evergreens for windy sites

Arbutus unedo
strawberry tree
Evergreen, with dark green serrated leaves, and white heatherlike flowers in autumn as bumpy red fruit ripens; cinnamon-colored bark. 25 × 25 ft. 'Compacta', to 15 × 15 ft. 'Elfin King', to 5 ft. Full sun to part shade. Zones 7-9.

Buxus 'Green Mountain'
boxwood
Upright habit; less likely to bronze in winter. 5 × 3 ft. Full sun to part shade. Zones 5-9.

Laurus nobilis
bay laurel
Fragrant, sturdy leaves. 15 × 15 ft. May grow larger in warm climates, up to 35 × 20 ft. Full sun. Zones 8–11.

Magnolia grandiflora
southern magnolia
Glossy green leaves with rusty brown undersides; saucer-sized, fragrant white flowers midspring and into summer. Not suitable for windy locations in more northern parts of its range. 60 × 50 ft. Smaller-growing selections include 'Little Gem', 20 × 10 ft.; 'St. Mary', 20 × 20 ft.; 'Victoria', 30 × 30 ft.; and 'Bracken's Brown Beauty', 30 × 25 ft. Full sun. Zones 6–10.

Magnolia virginiana
sweetbay magnolia
Evergreen to semi-evergreen, with white, fragrant flowers in late spring and sporadically through summer. 20 × 20 ft. Full sun to part shade. Zones 5–10.

Morella californica (syn. *Myrica californica*)
California wax myrtle
Evergreen, with narrow, aromatic leaves; vertical stems rise like pillars. Insignificant flowers followed by fruit attached directly to stem. Good wildlife habitat. Can be pruned to shape. 15 × 10 ft. Full sun. Zones 7–9.

Quercus virginiana
southern live oak
Evergreen or near-evergreen oak that develops long branches that sometimes reach to the ground; narrow leaves drop in spring when new growth begins. 60 × 100 ft. 'QVTIA' (Highrise), 40 × 25 ft., is easier to site but loses much of the poetry. Full sun. Zones 7–10.

Deciduous shrubs for windy sites

Cotinus coggygria
smoke bush
Round leaves, with airy flower heads that resemble plumes of smoke. Purple-leaved selections include 'Royal Purple', and C. *coggygria* × C. *obovatus* 'Grace'

has purple-red leaves. 'Golden Spirit' has chartreuse leaves. 12 × 12 ft. Full sun to part shade. Zones 5–8.

Potentilla fruticosa
cinquefoil
Small leaves. Flowers over a long period. Not for hot, humid climates. 'Abbottswood' has white flowers. 'Coronation Triumph' has bright yellow flowers. 4 × 4 ft. Full sun. Zones 2–8.

Spiraea japonica 'Gold Mound'
spirea
Golden foliage with yellow-red fall color. Clusters of pink flowers in summer. 3 × 4 ft. Full sun. Zones 4–8.

Viburnum plicatum f. *tomentosum*
doublefile viburnum
Horizontal branches with white spring flowers. 'Mariesii' and 'Shasta' are floriferous. 10 × 12 ft. Full sun to part shade. Zones 5–8.

THORNY PLANTS

Thorny plants help deter intrusion, so they can be planted as a single-species hedge, or you can include them in a hedgerow where they will knit together with other nonthorny plants to provide a barrier.

Shrubs and succulents

Agave parryi
artichoke agave
Blue-green succulent, with spine-tipped leaves. 4 × 5 ft. Flower stalks to 15 ft. Full sun. Zones 6–9.

Aralia spinosa
devil's walking stick
Deciduous; large compound leaves with spines on branches and leaf stems. Large clusters of flowers in spring followed by black fruit. 20 × 10 ft. Full sun to part shade. Zones 4–9.

Bougainvillea spp.
bougainvillea
Deciduous vine with colorful bracts in a wide range of colors. Many varieties, including 'Orange King', 'Miami Pink', and 'Scarlett O'Hara'. 30 ft. Full sun. Zones 10–11.

Eleutherococcus sieboldianus 'Variegatus'
(syn. *Acanthopanax sieboldianus* 'Variegatus')
variegated five-leaf aralia
Deciduous; creamy-edged foliage with short spines at leaf buds. Loose form can be sheared for hedge. 8 × 8 ft. Part shade. Zones 4–9.

Mahonia aquifolium (syn. *Berberis aquifolium*)
Oregon grape
Spreading evergreen with spine-tipped leaves; rounded spikes of fragrant yellow flowers in spring followed by blue fruit. 6 ft. Full sun to part shade. Zones 5–8. Related species *M. nervosa*, to 3 ft., forms thicket.

Mahonia ×*media* 'Charity'
Evergreen with long, horizontal, spine-tipped compound leaves. Fall spikes of yellow flowers are followed by blue fruit. Stems can be cut back or down to encourage new, lower growth. Asian mahonias provide fall and winter nectar for overwintering hummingbirds. 15 × 7 ft. 'Winter Sun', 10 × 4 ft. Part shade. Zones 7–9.

Opuntia santa-rita 'Tubac'
purple prickly pear
Evergreen cactus with prickly pads; new pads are purple tinged. 4 × 6 ft. Full sun. Zones 8–11.

Poncirus trifoliata
Japanese bitter orange
Deciduous; stems with 1 in. thorns. White fragrant flowers in spring. Yellow-orange fruit persists; bitter and seedy, but can be used for marmalade. 20 × 15 ft. Full sun. Zones 5–9.

Roses
Old-fashioned and native species roses often grow the best thorns; ramblers and large shrubs work well as barriers. These roses often bloom only once but may have showy hips that display throughout the rest of the year. Species native to coastal areas may tolerate salt spray.

North American native roses

Rosa nitida
shining rose
Bristly prickles and spines. Dark pink flowers followed by red berrylike hips. Good fall color. Grows well in wet sites. Native to American Northeast and eastern Canada. 3 ft. Full sun to part shade. Zones 6–9.

Rosa nutkana 'Plena' (syn. *R. californica*)
double-flowered Nootka rose
Deciduous, suckering, single-blooming, with fragrant, double-pink flowers in mid to late spring. Native to American Northwest. 8 × 8 ft. Full sun to part shade. Zones 3–9.

Rosa virginiana
Virginia rose
Deciduous, with prickly stems. Single-blooming, with fragrant pink, single flowers followed by red hips. Native to eastern North America. 6 × 6 ft. Full sun. Zones 3–9.

Other roses

Rosa 'Rambling Rector'
Deciduous and thorny. Semi-double white flowers with yellow centers in late spring. Rampant and floriferous with showy hips to follow. 20 × 20 ft. Full sun. Zones 5–9.

Rosa rugosa 'Scabrosa'
scabrosa rose
Deciduous, with bristly, spiny stems. Repeat flowering with fragrant, single, large magenta flowers followed by "tomato" hips. Tolerates poor soil. 5 × 6 ft. Full sun. Zones 2–9.

Rosa sericea subsp. omeiensis f. pteracantha
winged thorn rose
Deciduous, with translucent red thorns, especially on new growth. Vigorous upright growth. Single white flowers in spring. 8 × 7 ft. Full sun to part shade. Zones 6–9.

CRAB APPLES

A crab apple may be the ultimate garden plant for its ornamental and wildlife benefits. Spring blooms and colorful summer fruit that extends into fall or winter contributes to its beauty. Wildlife eat the fruit, which can be an especially important food source in the winter. Birds are attracted to the nectar in the flowers, and they eat the insects that in turn feed on flowers, foliage, and fruit. Crab apples also provide cross-pollination for other apple trees, and the larger fruits can be used to make jelly or cider.

At least eight crab apple species are native to North America, and you can find many varieties of disease-resistant, beautiful small trees to fit any garden. Note that native crab apples may be listed as genus *Malus* or *Pyrus*.

North American natives

Malus angustifolia
southern crab apple
Fragrant, late-spring flowers followed by small yellow fruit. Prefers moist to wet soil. Native to U.S. Southeast. 20 × 20 ft. Full sun. Zones 5–9.

Malus fusca
western crab apple
White to light pink flowers in spring; yellow or reddish fruit. Can form a thicket if left unpruned. Prefers moist to wet soil. Native to U.S. Pacific Northwest. Size is variable, up to 40 ft. Full sun. Zones 5–8.

Malus ioensis
prairie crab apple
Fragrant pink flowers in spring, followed by small yellow-green fruit. Native to U.S. Midwest and South. 35 × 30 ft. Full sun. Zones 4–8.

Disease-resistant hybrids

Several garden hybrids offer good disease resistance. All require full sun and are hardy in Zones 4–8.

'Adirondack' (syn. 'Admiration')
Red buds open to red-tinged, white flowers. Red-orange fruit is 1/2 in. diameter and persists to early winter. 18 × 10 ft.

'Evereste'
Red buds open to light pink flowers. Red-marked yellow fruit is 1 in. diameter; good size for cooking. 20 × 20 ft.

'Jewelcole' (Red Jewel)
White buds and flowers. Red fruit is 1/2 in. diameter and persistent. 15 × 12 ft.

'Prairifire'
Pink buds open to light pink flowers. Red fruit is 1/2 in. diameter and persistent. 20 × 20 ft.

'JFS-KW5' (Royal Raindrops)
Purple cut-leaf foliage. Red buds open to bright pink-red flowers. Red fruit is 1/4 in. diameter and persistent. 20 × 15 ft.

'Sutyzam' (Sugar Tyme)
Pale pink buds open to white flowers. Red fruit is 1/2 in. diameter and persistent. 18 × 15 ft.

Malus toringo subsp. *sargentii* 'Tina'
Dwarf form with deep pink buds that open to pink flowers. Red fruit is 1/4 in. diameter and persistent. 5 × 6 ft.

BROADLEAF EVERGREENS

In the coldest regions, broadleaf evergreens can be more trouble than benefit—heavy snow loads can break branches and even when there is no snow, cold, dry winds can suck moisture from plants. In general, with only few exceptions, these broadleaf evergreens will not thrive below Zone 6.

Arbutus unedo
strawberry tree
Dark green serrated leaves, and white heatherlike flowers in autumn as bumpy red fruit ripens; cinnamon-colored bark. 25 × 25 ft. 'Compacta', to 15 × 15 ft. 'Elfin King', to 5 ft. Full sun to part shade. Zones 7–9.

Ardisia escallonioides
marlberry
Spikes of white fragrant flowers appear throughout the year, with red fruit in spring. Florida native. 20 × 12 ft. Full sun to part shade. Zones 10–11.

Choisya ternata
Mexican orange
Clusters of lightly scented, white flowers in spring and fall. 8 × 8 ft. 'Sundance' (syn. 'Lich') has yellow leaves; *C ternata* ×*dewitteana* 'Aztec Pearl' has narrow leaves. 5 × 5 ft. Full sun. Zones 7–10.

Escallonia rubra
red escallonia
Evergreen, with small, rough leaves and clusters of small, tubular, red-pink flowers throughout the year, mostly in summer; can be sheared. 15 × 15 ft. Many hybrids and cultivars include rose-colored 'Pride of Donard', 5 × 8 ft., and 'Apple Blossom', 8 × 8 ft. Full sun. Zones 8–10.

Ilex ×*meserveae* 'Conapri' (Blue Princess)
blue holly
Spine-tipped leaves and small white flowers. Red fruit appears if male plant is present; use one male plant among several female plants for fruit set. 'Conablu'

(Blue Prince) and 'Mesan' (Blue Stallion) pollinate this selection. Other cultivars can be used the same way. 15 × 10 ft. Full sun to part shade. Zones 4–8.

Lantana camara
lantana
Deciduous; leaves feel rough; clusters of small, often two-toned flowers throughout summer are attractive to butterflies. 6 × 6 ft. Many other selections include 'American Red', to 6 ft. 'Miss Huff' is slightly more hardy, to 6 ft. Full sun. Zones 7–11.

Laurus nobilis
bay laurel
Fragrant, sturdy leaves. 15 × 15 ft. May grow larger in warm climates, up to 35 × 20 ft. Full sun. Zones 8–11.

Myrtus communis
common myrtle
Evergreen with dark green foliage; white fragrant flowers in summer, followed by blackish fruit. 12 × 12 ft. 'Compacta' is smaller, to 3 × 3 ft. Full sun. Zones 8–10. Related species *Luma apiculata* has flaky, cinnamon-colored bark, and may grow to 40 ft. but is usually more shrubby. Zones 8–11.

Osmanthus ×*burkwoodii*
hybrid sweet olive
Dark green foliage and fragrant white flowers in small clusters in spring. 8 × 8 ft. Full sun to part shade. Zones 7–9.

Phillyrea angustifolia
false olive
Narrow leaves and insignificant flowers. Good informal or trimmed hedge. 10 × 10 ft. Full sun to part shade. Zones 7–9.

Photinia ×*fraseri*
redtip
Glossy foliage with copper-red new growth. Mounds of tiny cream-colored flowers in spring. Fungal leaf spot can be problematic. 15 × 15 ft. Full sun to part shade. Zones 7–9.

Pieris japonica
lily of the valley shrub
Whorls of new leaves are bronze-red, with clusters of lightly fragrant, pink-tinged heatherlike flowers in early spring. Broadly spreading shrub can be limbed up to reveal shredding bark. 12 × 8 ft. Smaller cultivars available. Full sun to part shade. Zones 5–8.

Pittosporum tenuifolium
pittosporum
Small, wavy-margined leaves with black stems. Late spring flowers small but fragrant. Can be trimmed for hedge. 30 × 15 ft. Smaller-growing cultivars include 'Garnetii', with white leaf margins, 15 × 12 ft., and 'Purpureum', to 10 × 5 ft. Full sun to part shade. Zones 8–11.

Prunus carolinana
Carolina cherry laurel
Glossy foliage. Fragrant, white late-winter flowers followed by black fruit. 40 × 20 ft. Full sun to part shade. Zones 7–9.

Prunus laurocerasus
English cherry laurel
Large, glossy leaves. Upright clusters of white flowers in spring followed by black fruit. 30 × 30 ft. Full sun to part shade. Zones 6–8.

Prunus lusitanica
Portuguese laurel
Dark, glossy leaves with red stems. Upright clusters of white flowers followed by red fruit. 30 × 30 ft. Full sun to part shade. Zones 7–9.

Ternstroemia gymnanthera (syn. *T. japonica*)
cleyera
Glossy leaves with bronze-red new growth. White flowers, with some berry set in autumn. Often sheared. 12 × 8 ft. Part to full shade. Zones 7–9.

Vaccinium ovatum
evergreen huckleberry
Evergreen, with pink spring flowers and black, edible summer fruit. 5 × 5 ft. Taller growth in shade. Part shade to shade. Zones 7–9.

Viburnum 'Pragense'
Prague viburnum
Dark, elliptic leaves. Clusters of lightly fragrant, white flowers develop into black fruit. 12 × 12 ft. Full sun to part shade. Zones 5–8.

NO-SHEAR HEDGE PLANTS

Several compact-growing evergreens can provide a short or long hedge without requiring continual maintenance to keep them in bounds.

Juniperus chinensis 'Kaizuka' (syn. 'Tortulosa')
Chinese juniper
Conifer with dark green foliage. Upper branches ascending, and they twist. 15 × 10 ft. 'Spartan', 25 × 8 ft. Full sun. Zones 4–9.

Juniperus virginiana
eastern red cedar
Conifer with blue-green foliage. Alternate host for apple cedar rust; do not plant near orchards. 'Burkii', 25 × 10 ft. 'Canaertti', 25 × 15 ft. 'Cupressifolia', 15 × 8 ft. 'Emerald Sentinel', 20 × 8 ft. Full sun. Zones 4–9.

Taxus baccata 'Standishii'
English yew
Conifer with bright golden foliage. Sun to part shade. Prefers moist, well-drained soil. 7 × 3 ft. Zones 5–8.

Thuja occidentalis
arborvitae
Conifer with medium to dark green foliage. 'Brandon', 15 × 8 ft. 'DeGroot's Spire', 30 × 6 ft. 'Holmstrup', 10 × 3 ft. 'Nigra', dark green foliage; good choice for cold climates, 30 × 10 ft. 'Smaragd', 15 × 4 ft. 'Techny', 15 × 8 ft. 'Wintergreen', 30 × 10 ft. Zones 3–8, except humid regions.

NARROW PLANTS

If only breeders would develop a plant that would grow as wide and as high as we tell it to grow. Until genetic engineering splices some auditory instruction-following DNA into a maple's genes, gardeners must look for the right piece of the puzzle to provide a plant screen for tight spots. The possibilities, not endless, offer choices for almost any landscape. Narrow plants mostly have ascending branches, but a few grow short side branches that hold close to the trunk.

Berberis thunbergii f. *atropurpurea* 'Helmond Pillar'
barberry
Deciduous upright thorny shrub with dark purple-red foliage; begins narrow, but develops middle-age spread. 4 × 4 ft. *B. thunbergii* 'Maria' stays narrow, to 3 ft. Full sun. Zones 4–8.

Buxus sempervirens 'Monrue'
boxwood
Evergreen shrub with some bronzing in cold winters. 9 × 2 ft. 'Green Mountain', 5 × 3 ft. Full sun to part shade. Zones 5–9. 'Graham Blandy' is greener, 8 × 2 ft. Sun to shade. Zones 6–8.

Calamagrostis ×*acutiflora* 'Overdam'
silver reed grass
Herbaceous grass, with variegated, narrow leaves. Suffers in humidity. Cut down at winter's end. 'Karl Foerster' similar without variegation. 5 × 2 ft. Full sun. Zones 4–9.

Cedrus atlantica 'Glauca Pendula'
weeping blue atlas cedar
Evergreen conifer with blue-gray foliage and weeping habit. Can be trained to create a curtain of foliage. 10 × 20 ft. Full sun. Zones 6–8.

Chamaecyparis lawsoniana 'Blue Surprise'
Port Orford cedar
Blue-tinted conifer; needs protection from hot afternoon sun in warm climates. 6 × 2 ft. Full sun. Zones 6–9.

Cupressus sempervirens
Italian cypress
Conifer with short, mostly horizontal or slightly ascending branches. Look for Stricta Group for narrowest form. 60 × 6 ft. 'Swane's Golden', golden yellow new growth, 20 × 3 ft. 'Tiny Tower', 25 × 3 ft. Full sun. Zones 7–10.

Enkianthus campanulatus
red-veined enkianthus
Deciduous shrub with good fall color. Early spring clusters of bell-shaped flowers. Prefers evenly moist soil. 8 × 6 ft. Full sun to part shade. Zones 5–8.

Euonymus japonicus 'Green Spire'
evergreen euonymus
Evergreen shrub with small, serrated leaves; good for a green wall. 8 × 2 ft. Full sun to part shade. Zones 6–9.

Fagus sylvatica 'Dawyck'
European beech
Deciduous; upright habit. Not for dry hot or humid hot regions. Plant a group of three for better effect. Also available in purple ('Dawyck Purple') and gold ('Dawyck Gold'). 80 × 10 ft. Sun to part shade. Zones 4–8.

Fagus sylvatica 'Red Obelisk' (syn. 'Rohan Obelisk')
European beech
Red deciduous foliage. Slow-growing. For the beech hedge that needs no pruning. 40 × 3 ft. Sun to part shade. Zones 4–8.

Ilex crenata 'Sky Pencil'
Japanese holly
Evergreen, small-leaved shrub; vertical branches can splay slightly at top. Plant close together for best coverage. 10 × 1 ft. Full sun to part shade. Zones 5–8.

Ilex vomitoria 'Will Fleming'
yaupon holly
Evergreen with small leaves. Withstands low water, poor soil. Similar habit as fastigiated yew when grown against a house. 15 × 2 ft. Full sun. Zones 5–8.

Juniperus scopulorum 'Skyrocket'
Rocky Mountain juniper
Conifer with blue-green foliage. Requires good drainage. 20 × 3 ft. 'Medora' is very blue, 10 × 3 ft. Full sun. Zones 4-9.

Juniperus virginiana 'Blue Arrow'
eastern red cedar
Blue-green conifer, good for the low-water landscape. 15 × 2 ft. Full sun. Zones 4-9.

Juniperus virginiana 'Monbell'
eastern red cedar
Conifer with silver-blue foliage and short side branches. 20 × 3 ft. Full sun. Zones 4-9.

Juniperus virginiana 'Taylor'
eastern red cedar
Conifer with blue-green, compact foliage. Good substitute for Italian cypress in cold climates. 30 × 3 ft. Full sun. Zones 3-9.

Nandina domestica
heavenly bamboo
Evergreen shrub with narrow leaves and colorful foliage. 'Plum Passion' has purple foliage. 5 × 4 ft. Sun to shade. Zones 6-9.

Picea orientalis 'Skylands'
oriental spruce
Conifer with yellow-tinted foliage. 35 × 12 ft. Full sun to part shade. Zones 5-8.

Pinus sylvatica 'Fastigiata'
Scots pine
Conifer with blue-green needles and reddish, fissured bark. Tolerant of urban pollution. 20 × 4 ft. Full sun. Zones 2-8.

Podocarpus macrophyllus 'Maki'
yew pine
Evergreen conifer with narrow leaves instead of needles. Good for humid regions. 10 × 4 ft. Full sun to part shade. Zones 7-10.

Rhamnus frangula 'Ron Williams'
buckthorn
Deciduous shrub with ferny look. Not associated with the invasive species. 7 × 2 ft. Full sun to part shade. Zones 2-8.

Rosmarinus officianalis 'Arp'
rosemary
Evergreen herb, with fragrant leaves. Tolerates shearing and clipping. 6 × 4 ft. Full sun to part shade. Zones 6-10.

Sciadopitys verticillata 'Joe Kozey'
Japanese umbrella pine
Whorls of soft, dark green needles. 12 × 2 ft. Full sun to part shade. Zones 5-9.

Taxus ×media 'Hicksii'
Hick's yew
Evergreen shrub with dark, needlelike leaves. Tolerates shearing. 20 × 6 ft. 'Bean Pole', 10 × 4 ft. 'Flushing', 16 × 3 ft. Full sun to part shade. Zones 4-8.

Xanthocyparis nootkatensis 'Green Arrow'
(syn. *Chamaecyparis nootkatensis*)
Alaska cedar
Upswept, irregular branches with droopy leader. Makes a great exclamation point. 30 × 5 ft. Full sun. Zones 4-8.

SMALL TREES

Trees of any size add to the biodiversity of the garden and offer a place where birds and insects find nesting space, food, and shelter. The balance of nature can be achieved even in small spaces where a variety of plant materials exist. Using one small tree creates an accent, and using several in various ways helps create a cohesive garden design with repetition and sequencing.

Before you plant, be sure the tree is the best one to meet your needs, and consider its requirements, size, and shape: shade or sun, short and wide, or tall and narrow. Many of these suggestions are as wide or wider than tall. One spreading tree will give you the most coverage for your canopy. Consider deciduous trees when you need a screen only in late spring into autumn.

Acer buergerianum
trident maple
Deciduous, with trilobed leaves, yellow winged seed-pods, and good fall color. 30 × 30 ft. Full sun. Zones 5-9.

Acer campestre
hedge maple
Deciduous, with dark green, shallowly lobed leaves. Good shearing hedge plant. 25 × 25 ft. Full sun to part shade. Zones 5-8.

Acer griseum
paperbark maple
Deciduous, with leaves in groups of three, with orange and red fall color. Curling cinnamon-colored bark. Slow growing. 40 × 30 ft. Full sun to part shade. Zones 5-8.

Acer palmatum
Japanese maple
Deciduous, with pointed-lobed leaves. Hundreds of specialty cultivars are available, but seed-grown plants make inexpensive and beautiful trees. Buy in autumn from a nursery to choose the best fall color. 30 × 30 ft. Full sun to part shade. Zones 6-8.

Acer tartaricum subsp. *ginnala* (syn. *A. ginnala*)
Amur maple
Deciduous, with bright red fall color and fragrant flow-ers. Sometime multi-trunked. 20 × 20 ft. Full sun to part shade. Zones 2-8.

Amelanchier ×*grandiflora* 'Autumn Brilliance'
serviceberry
Deciduous, with clusters of strappy white flowers followed by blue berries. Red fall color. Often multi-stemmed, which lends an elegant look. Other selec-tions include 'Princess Diana' and 'Robin Hill'. 25 × 15 ft. Full sun. Zones 4-9.

Betula nigra 'Little King'
river birch
Deciduous, with white, peeling bark. 12 × 12 ft. Full sun to part shade. Zones 4-9.

Betula nigra 'Studetec' (Tecumseh Compact)
spreading river birch
Deciduous, with white, peeling bark. Useful as low screen. 12 × 20 ft. Full sun to part shade. Zones 4-9.

Calliandra haematocephala
powderpuff tree
Deciduous, with compound leaves and pink or red puffy summer flowers. Foliage and flowers provide fine overall texture. 5 × 15 ft. Full sun. Zones 9-11.

Carpinus betulus 'Frans Fontaine'
European hornbeam
Deciduous tree stays more narrow than 'Fastigiata'. Can be formed into arches or trained as stilt hedge. 30 × 15 ft. Full sun. Zones 4-8.

Carpinus caroliniana
American hornbeam
Deciduous, with serrated leaves in nature and smooth gray bark. An understory tree, so it will tolerate shade. 30 × 30 ft. Sun to shade. Zones 3-9.

Carpinus japonica
Japanese hornbeam
Deciduous, with neatly pleated leaves and red leaf stems. 30 × 25 ft. Full sun to part shade. Zones 4-9.

Cercidiphyllum japonicum
katsura
Deciduous. Fall foliage smells like caramel. 40 × 30 ft. Full sun to part shade. Zones 4-8.

Chilopsis linearis
desert willow
Deciduous tree, with pink, funnel-shaped, scented flowers throughout summer. Round form makes a good screen. Seedpods can be messy. 25 × 25 ft. Full sun. Zones 7-10.

×*Chitalpa tashkentensis*
desert willow
Deciduous, cross of *Catalpa bignonioides* ×*Chilopsis linearis*, with pink funnel-shaped flowers in summer. Will tolerate cold temperatures. 25 × 25 ft. Full sun. Zones 6–8.

Cornus kousa var. *chinensis*
Chinese dogwood
Deciduous, with red fall leaves. Large white flowers in mid to late spring, followed by red fruit. Disease-resistant. *C. kousa* 'Miss Satomi' has pink flowers. 25 × 25 ft. Full sun. Zones 4–8.

Fagus sylvatica 'Dawyck'
European beech
Deciduous; upright habit. Not for dry hot or humid hot regions. Plant a group of three for better effect. Also available in purple ('Dawyck Purple') and gold ('Dawyck Gold'). 80 × 10 ft. Sun to part shade. Zones 4–8.

Ginkgo biloba 'Princeton Sentry'
Deciduous, with fan-shaped, green leaves that turn bright yellow in the fall. Male trees produce catkins in spring and females produce messy, odorous seed pods. 50 × 30 ft. Other male cultivars with distinct shapes include 'Fastigiata', 50 × 15 ft., and 'Jade Butterflies', 12 × 9 ft. Full sun. Zones 3–8.

Halesia caroliniana (syn. *H. tetraptera*)
Carolina silverbell
Deciduous, with white, bell-shaped flowers in mid-spring. Tolerates shade from larger trees. 30 × 20 ft. Full sun to part shade. Zones 4–8.

Ilex ×*attenuata* 'Fosteri'
Foster's holly
Evergreen. Cross of two American natives, *I. cassine* × *I. opaca*. Red berries. *I.* ×*attenuata* 'Sunny Foster' has yellow foliage, especially new growth. 30 × 15 ft. Full sun to part shade. Zones 6–9.

Koelreuteria paniculata
goldenrain tree
Deciduous, with midsummer yellow flowers and pink seedpods. 30 × 30 ft. Full sun to part shade. Zones 6–9.

Nyssa sylvatica
tupelo
Deciduous, with red, orange, and yellow fall color. 40 × 20 ft. Full sun to part shade. Zones 4–8.

Oxydendrum arboreum
sourwood
Deciduous, with glossy green leaves that turn bright orange in autumn. White summer flowers appear in fingerlike clusters. Native to the American Southeast and tolerant of both wet and (when established) dry soils. 25 × 15 ft. Full sun to part shade. Zones 5–9.

Pistacia chinensis
Chinese pistachio
Deciduous, with red-orange fall color. Tolerates heat. 30 × 30 ft. Full sun. Zones 4–9.

Pittosporum tobira
Japanese mock orange
Evergreen with spoon-shaped leaves; clusters of fragrant white flowers in early spring. Grows best and largest in mild, warm climates. 'Variegata' has white-edged leaves. 15 × 18 ft. Full sun. Zones 8–10.

Ptelea trifoliata
hop tree
Deciduous, with dark green leaves and unshowy flowers. Tough tree but flowers and bruised foliage have unpleasant smell, so site it at the far corner of the garden. 20 × 20 ft. Part shade to shade. Zones 4–9.

Quercus robur 'Fastigiata' (Skyrocket)
fastigiate English oak
Deciduous, with narrow, oval growth habit. 45 × 15 ft. Full sun. Zones 4–8.

Stewartia pseudocamellia
Japanese stewartia
Deciduous, with white summer flowers, bright fall color, and mottled pink, tan, and gray bark. Elegant in all seasons. Best for an understory tree; keep out of the heat. 25 × 12 ft. Alternatives include orangebark stewartia (*S. monadelpha*) and American native mountain stewartia (*S. ovata*), to 15 ft. Part shade. Zones 5–8.

Styrax obassia
fragrant snowbell
Deciduous, with large leaves and reddish bark. In late spring, chains of pendant, fragrant, white flowers with yellow stamens appear. 20 × 20 ft. Full sun to part shade. Zones 5–8. Grow in a protected area in Zone 5.

Trochodendron aralioides
wheel tree
Evergreen. Leaves are whorled. Flowers appear in creamy spikes. Horizontal branches create a tiered effect. 20 × 15 ft. Full sun to part shade. Zones 6–8.

Xanthoceras sorbifolium
yellowhorn
Deciduous, with compound, glossy leaves. White spring flowers with red centers. Unusual large shrub or small tree for warm, protected place. 15 × 8 ft. Full sun. Zones 6–9.

Zelkova serrata 'Village Green'
Japanese zelkova
Deciduous; leaves persist on tree through winter months. Begins vase shaped and matures to a round crown. 40 × 40 ft. Full sun to part shade. Zones 5–9.

VINES FOR TRELLISES

Vines can be trained to wind back and forth through a length of trellis for more coverage. Several selections offer good coverage.

Actinidia kolomikta
male hardy kiwi
Deciduous, twining vine. Leaves irregularly and boldly marked with white and pink. Shear lightly in late winter for fuller foliage. 18 ft. Bright shade. Zones 5–8.

Campsis radicans
trumpet vine
Deciduous, with compound leaves and orange trumpet-shaped flowers in summer. Aerial roots adhere to surface. Aggressive grower. American native. 40 ft. More compact (to 15 ft.) selections include 'Apricot' and *C. radicans* f. *flava*. Hybrid *C.* ×*tagliabuana* 'Madame Galen' has watermelon-colored flowers, to 25 ft. Relative of cross vine (*Bignonia capreolata*), to 50 ft., with orange flowers. Full sun. Zones 4–9.

Ficus pumila
creeping fig
Evergreen clinging vine. 15 ft. Part shade. Zones 9–11.

Gelsemium sempervirens
Carolina jasmine
Evergreen, twining vine with glossy narrow leaves. Clusters of yellow, funnel-shaped, fragrant flowers cover the plant in late winter and early spring. Semi-evergreen in its northern range in the United States. Native to American Southeast. 20 ft. Full sun. Zones 7–10.

Humulus lupus 'Aureus'
golden hop vine
Herbaceous twining vine with golden yellow foliage. Hoplike flowers appear in late summer. Easier to manage when grown alone on a trellis. 25 ft. Full sun to part shade. Zones 3–8.

Hydrangea anomala subsp. *petiolaris*
climbing hydrangea
Deciduous, with glossy green leaves. Lacecap white flowers in late spring. Adheres to surfaces using aerial roots. Peeling bark on older stems and short horizontal branches add to winter interest. 30–60 ft. Part shade. Zones 4–8.

Parthenocissus henryana
silvervein creeper vine
Deciduous, with whorled leaves that begin bronze-red in color, mature with a pewter-colored midvein, and become orange and scarlet in fall. Adheres using pads. Most shade-tolerant of creeper vines. Can be pulled off structure and cut back hard. 30 ft. Full sun to full shade. Zones 6–9.

Passiflora incarnata
maypop, purple passionflower
Deciduous, with glossy leaves and lavender flowers throughout the summer. May die to ground in colder regions. Native to American Southeast. *P. caerulea* is from South America. 10 ft. Full sun to part shade. Zones 5–9.

Rosa banksiae var. *banksiae*
white Lady Banks' rose
Evergreen with nearly thornless stems; blooms once in spring, with clusters of small, fragrant, double-white flowers. 'Lutea' has yellow, lightly scented flowers. 20–50 ft. Full sun. Zones 8–10.

Rosa 'John Davis'
Deciduous climbing rose with red stems and double-pink flowers. Arching stems can add height to a fence. 7 × 8 ft. Full sun. Zones 3–8.

Rosa 'William Baffin'
Deciduous pillar rose with double-pink flowers in late spring through summer. Arching stems can add height to a fence. 10 × 6 ft. Full sun. Zones 3–9.

Schizophragma hydrangeoides
Japanese hydrangea vine
Deciduous, with large, heart-shaped leaves. Clusters of white flowers are similar to climbing hydrangea; teardrop-shaped "petals" form an irregular halo around center. 'Moonlight' has a pewter-colored pattern on leaves. 6 × 30 ft. Part shade to shade. Zones 5–8.

Thunbergia alata
black-eyed Susan vine
Evergreen twining vine, with yellow, orange, or red flowers with black eyes. Grown as a half-hardy annual in colder regions. 20 ft. Full sun to part shade. Zones 10–11.

Vitis coignetiae
crimson glory vine
Deciduous, with heart-shaped leaves that turn crimson in fall. Attaches by tendrils once established. Cutting vine to the ground produces extra-large leaves. 20–60 ft. Full sun to part shade. Zones 5–9.

CONVERSION TABLES AND PLANT HARDINESS ZONES

LENGTH

inches	cm
1/4	0.6
1/3	0.8
1/2	1.3
3/4	1.9
1	2.5
2	5.1
3	7.6
4	10
5	13
6	15
7	18
8	20
9	23
10	25
20	51
30	76
40	100

feet	m
1	0.3
2	0.6
3	0.9
4	1.2
5	1.5
6	1.8
7	2.1
8	2.4
9	2.7
10	3
20	6
30	9
40	12

TEMPERATURES

$$°C = 5/9 \times (°F - 32)$$
$$°F = (9/5 \times °C) + 32$$

WEIGHT

1 oz.	28 grams
1 lb.	454 grams

PLANT HARDINESS ZONES
Average Annual Minimum Temperature

Zone	Temperature (deg. F)	Temperature (deg. C)
1	Below −50	Below −46
2	−50 to −40	−46 to −40
3	−40 to −30	−40 to −34
4	−30 to −20	−34 to −29
5	−20 to −10	−29 to −2
6	−10 to 0	−23 to −18
7	0 to 10	−18 to −12
8	10 to 20	−12 to −7
9	20 to 30	−7 to −1
10	30 to 40	−1 to 4
11	40 and above	4 and above

To see the U.S. Department of Agriculture Hardiness Zone Map, go to the U.S. National Arboretum site at http://www.usna.usda.gov/Hardzone/ushzmap.html.

RESOURCES

AltruWood
www.altrucedar.com
Information on sustainably harvested Western red cedar products

Amazon.com
www.amazon.com
Source of garden trellises and other structures

American Bamboo Society
www.americanbamboo.org
Information on bamboo, its culture, and its uses

Arbor Day Foundation
www.arborday.org
Tree selection, tree planting practices, hardiness zones, and tree facts for all ages

Benjamin Moore
www.benjaminmoore.com
Low volatile organic compounds (VOC) paint

Craigslist
www.craigslist.org
Recycled materials for building and garden projects from local businesses and people

The Deer-Shock Depot
www.electric-deer-fence.com
Electric deer fence products

Eastern Red Cedar Products
www.cedarusa.com
Information on the use of *Juniperus virginiana* lumber in the landscape

Federal Highway Administration
www.fhwa.dot.gov/environment/keepdown.htm
Information about highway traffic noise barriers

Forest Farm
www.forestfarm.com
Source for hedgerow plants and plants for windy and salty sites

Forest Stewardship Council
www.fscus.org and www.fsc-uk.org
Wood products certified by the FSC are grown and harvested with the least impact on the environment.

Garden-Fountains.com
www.garden-fountains.com
Water features and information on garden fountains

Gardener's Supply Company
www.Gardeners.com
Water features, information on garden fountains, trellises, and tips for excluding pests from the garden

GardenSite
www.gardensite.co.uk
Trellises and other garden structures

Hedges Direct
www.hedgesdirect.co.uk
A source for hedgerow plants and plants for windy and salty sites

Home Depot
www.homedepot.com
FSC wood for fencing

International Society of Arboriculture
www.treesaregood.org
Information on why and how to plant trees

Juniper Works
www.westcoastjuniper.com
Sustainable western juniper for fencing

Lady Bird Johnson Wildflower Center
www.wildflower.org
The center's native plant database lets you search for native plants by name or by region.

Livos
www.livos.co.uk
Natural paints

Lowe's
www.lowes.com
FSC wood

North American Native Plant Society
www.nanps.org
Information and education about native plants, plus a connection to your local native plant society

NW Sustainable Building Products
www.nwsbp.com
Sustainable western juniper fencing

The Old Fashioned
Milk Paint Company
www.milkpaint.com
Milk-based, environmentally
friendly paint

Rawnsley Woodland Products
www.cornishwoodland.co.uk
FSC Western red cedar and
redwood materials

The Real Milk Paint Co.
www.realmilkpaint.com
Milk-based, environmentally
friendly paint

Redwood Empire
www.redwoodemp.com
FSC Sequoia products

Sherwin-Williams
www.sherwin-williams.com
Low-VOC paint

Trellis Structures
www.trellisstructures.com
Trellises and other garden
structures

Wind & Weather
www.windandweather.com
Garden fountains and other
outdoor water features

UKWaterfeatures.com
www.ukwaterfeatures.com
Garden fountains and other
outdoor water features

84 Lumber
www.84lumber.com
FSC wood

FURTHER READING

Barthel, Thomas. 2010.
*Dogscaping: Creating the Perfect
Backyard and Garden for You and
Your Dog.* BowTie Press: Irvine,
California.

Beneke, Jeff. 2005.
*The Fence Bible: How to plan,
build, and install fences and gates
to meet every home style and
property need, no matter what size
your yard.* Storey Publishing: North
Adams, Massachusetts.

Buckland, Toby. 2003.
*Garden Boundaries: 20 Projects
for Trellises, Walls, Fences, Gates,
Screens, and Hedges.* Laurel Glen
Publishing: San Diego, California.

Duchscherer, Paul,
and Douglas Keister. 1999.
*Outside the Bungalow: America's
Arts & Crafts Garden.* Penguin
Studio: New York.

Dunnett, Nigel, and Noel Kingsbury.
2008. *Planting Green Roofs and
Living Walls.* Timber Press: Portland, Oregon.

Smith, Cheryl S. 2004.
*Dog Friendly Gardens, Garden
Friendly Dogs,* Dogwise Publishing:
Wenatchee, Washington.

Sunset, ed. 1997. *Sunset National
Garden Book.* Sunset Books, Inc:
Menlo Park, California.

Tallamy, Douglas W. 2009.
*Bringing Nature Home: How You
Can Sustain Wildlife With Native
Plants.* Timber Press: Portland,
Oregon.

Williamson, Tom. 2002.
Hedges and Walls (Living Land-
scapes series). The National Trust:
London.

ACKNOWLEDGMENTS

This book owes its existence to the many people standing alongside the author, including the host of gardeners who, over the years, asked many questions. I hope that this book will provide many answers.

My thanks to Garden Bench Books for helping get this book idea off the ground. Thanks to the designers who shared not only their ideas, but example photos of their fabulous work: Daniel Lowery of Queen Anne Gardens (photos by Tristin Brown), queenannegardens.com; Cameron Scott, Betsy Anderson, and other designers from Exteriorscapes, www.exteriorscapes.com; Kathy and Tim King of Land2c Landscape Design, www.Land2c.com; Octavia Chambliss, octaviachambliss.com; and Lee Neff.

The professional photographers who contributed to the book show not only technical skill, but also an excellent eye for plants and good gardens.

Thanks to Timber Press editors and designers, who see garden and plant topics as the ultimate in book publishing.

Books are as much a work of the author's family and friends as the author herself, so thanks to all who have questioned, answered, or just listened to me think out loud during the creation of this book.

PHOTO AND DESIGN CREDITS

Photo credits

Tristin Brown: pages 45 top, 80 bottom right

Andrew Buchanan/SLP: frontispiece, pages 23 bottom left, 28 top, 29, 33, 36, 36, 47, 50–51, 52, 68, 73 bottom, 75, 94, 95 right, 106, 110 top right, 112 left

Karen Bussolini: pages 10, 28 bottom, 32, 42, 45 bottom, 59 bottom, 95 left, 97, 101, 102 bottom right, 107, 122

Rob Cardillo: pages 6, 8–9, 65, 67 bottom right, 69, 76 bottom, 79, 82 top right, 102 top, 110 bottom, 115, 121

Alan & Linda Detrick Photography: pages 13, 119

Andrew Drake: pages 20, 34 top left, 71 right, 91 left, 91 right, 112 right

Virginia Hand: pages 30, 39, 55 top right and bottom, 56, 67 bottom left, 76 top left, 78, 86, 90, 99, 102 bottom left, 105 top left, 108 left

Joshua McCullough, PhytoPhoto: page 27

John Neff: page 83

Rich Pomerantz: pages 64 top, 82 top left, 111

Cameron Scott: pages 34 bottom, 64 bottom, 71 left, 80 bottom left, 105 bottom, 108 right, 110 top left

Ellen Spector Platt: pages 60 bottom, 118

Mark Turner: pages 16–17, 18, 23 bottom right and top, 24, 40, 55 top left, 59 top, 60 top, 63, 67 top, 70, 73 top left and right, 74, 80 top, 88, 98, 105 top right

Leighton Wingate: page 156

Emily Zulauf: page 46

Design credits

Octavia Chambliss: page 46

Classic Courtyards: page 101 right

Dickson DeMarche: page 97 top

Scot Eckley: pages 33, 50–51, 68, 110 top right, 112 left

Exteriorscapes: pages 34 bottom, 64 bottom, 71 left, 80 bottom left, 105 bottom, 108 right, 110 top left

Juanita Flagg: page 97 bottom

Inta Krombolz: page 28 bottom, 95 left, 102 bottom right

Land2c Landscape Design: pages 34 top right, 49, 76 top right, 93, 117

Carole Ottesen: page 101 left

Martha Petersen/Neil Jorgensen: page 107

Plantscapes: page 32

Queen Anne Gardens LLC: pages 45 top, 80 bottom right

Paul and Moira Sakren: page 45 bottom

Swamp Fox Gardens: page 10

Dr. Gordon White and James David: page 42

INDEX

ABOUT THE AUTHOR

Marty Wingate is a Seattle-based writer and speaker about gardens and travel. She is the author of three other books: *The Bellevue Botanical Garden: Celebrating 15 Years*, *Big Ideas for Northwest Small Gardens*, and *The Big Book of Northwest Perennials*.

Marty writes plant articles for *Landscape Architecture* magazine and contributes to other national publications including *American Gardener*, *Country Gardens*, *and Gardening How-to*. She volunteers on the editorial board of the Washington Park Arboretum Bulletin, and is a weekly guest on the Greendays segment on KUOW (94.9 FM), Seattle's NPR station.

Marty has a master's degree in urban horticulture from the University of Washington and is active in the Arboretum Foundation, the Northwest Horticultural Society, the Royal Horticultural Society, and the Garden Writers Association. She leads garden tours to England, Scotland, and Ireland, and North American destinations. Her website is martywingate.com.